PELICAN BOOKS

THE FIRST CIVILIZATIONS

Dr Glyn Daniel is Fellow and Director of Studies in Archaeology and Anthropology at St John's College, Cambridge, and lecturer in archaeology in the University. He is Editor of the quarterly journal *Antiquity* and of a series of books entitled *Ancient Peoples and Places*. His main interests in archaeology are megalithic monuments, prehistoric art, the archaeology of Western Europe and the Mediterranean, and the history of archaeology. He has published many books on these subjects, including *The Megalith Builders of Western Europe*, *The Idea of Prehistory* and *The Origins and Growth of Archaeology* (all in Pelicans). A frequent broadcaster on sound radio and television, he is at present adviser to *Chronicle* and B.B.C. 2, and a director of Anglia Television. He is a director of the Arts Theatre at Cambridge and a trustee of the Museum of London. He has written two detective stories, *The Cambridge Murders* and *Welcome Death*, which are published in Penguins. He is advisory editor in archaeology to Penguin Books.

D0726930

GLYN DANIEL

THE FIRST CIVILIZATIONS

THE
ARCHAEOLOGY
OF THEIR
ORIGINS

PENGUIN BOOKS

Penguin Books Ltd, Harmondsworth, Middlesex, England
Penguin Books Australia Ltd, Ringwood, Victoria, Australia

—

First published by Thames & Hudson 1968
Published in Pelican Books 1971
Copyright © Glyn Daniel 1968

—

Made and printed in Great Britain by
C. Nicholls & Company Ltd
Set in Linotype Granjon

To Frank and Jane

CONTENTS

LIST OF PLATES

FIGURES IN THE TEXT

SOURCES OF ILLUSTRATIONS

	SUMER	EGYPT	INDUS	CHINA	AMERICA — SOUTH	AMERICA — NORTH
1500 A.D.					Inca Empire	
1000 A.D.					Coastal states, Chimú Empire	Yucatán
500 A.D.						End of Maya Teotihuacán destroyed
A.D./B.C.		30 Egypt a Roman Province · 196 Rosetta Stone		HAN		
500 B.C.	516 Behistun Inscription · 612 Nineveh sacked · Sargon II (721–705)	LATE PERIOD		LATE · EARLY — C H O U	Chavín	Olmecs at La Venta
1000 B.C.		NEW KINGDOM		1122 · 1384 Anyang founded — LATE · MIDDLE · EARLY	First ceremonial centres	Ceremonial centres on Gulf Coast (Olmecs)
1500 B.C.		MIDDLE KINGDOM	?Destruction Mohenjo-daro, Harappa, Kot Diji, Lothal, etc.	S H A N G		
2000 B.C.	Sargon of Akkad		INDUS VALLEY CIVILIZATION	PROTO- · ↑ Yang Shao		Village life in Mexico
2500 B.C.	URUK I — EARLY DYNASTIC I II III	DYN.IV Giza Pyramid	?			
3000 B.C.	Royal Graves of Ur · II — URUK	DYN.III Step Pyramid · DYN.I Narmer — OLD KINGDOM			Fishing and cultivation in Peru	
3500 B.C.	Jemdet Nasr · V · XIV	PREDYNASTIC · ARCHAIC				
4000 B.C.	Hajji Muhammad — ?UBAID EARLY/LATE	XVIII			Hunters and gatherers	

PREFACE

THIS book is based on eight lectures given in the University of East Anglia in Norwich in the Michaelmas Term of 1965, and repeated afterwards in the University of Cambridge. A summary version of them was broadcast in the Third Programme of the British Broadcasting Corporation in the spring of 1967 and the text of these summaries was published in the *Listener*.

This course of lectures was the first series of public lectures given in the University of East Anglia which started in 1961; and in planning it with the Vice-Chancellor, my friend and colleague Frank Thistlethwaite, we decided that while we should try to attract as wide an audience as possible from both inside and outside the University, we should provide a course which demanded some thought and concentration on the part of the audience. It is all too easy, as every archaeological lecturer knows only too well, to produce a popular lecture with the aid of slides showing buried treasures, strange scientific techniques, history emerging from the ground. We wanted in this series to use the popularity of archaeology to direct the serious attention of people interested in man's past to this one central problem: what light can archaeology throw on the origins of civilizations?

We did not know what reception they would have. There

might have been nobody there, or a large inquiring audience on the first night and nobody afterwards. In fact, all eight lectures were given to a very large audience. I hope that, in their present form, they will reach that far wider audience of non-professional archaeologists and historians for whom they are intended. This is not a book for specialists; my professional colleagues will find mistakes of fact and interpretation in every line, if they are so inclined. These lectures were given to non-specialists, to ordinary university students reading physics or geology or Romance literature, to ordinary people – housewives, bus-conductors – the man who drives me in a taxi in Norwich, and the man who cooks me spring rolls and barbecued spare-rib in the Chinese Restaurant.

But in my Norwich audiences there were serious students anxious to take the matters I discussed further by conversation and by reading, and so after most of the lectures we held seminars where points summarily mentioned in the lectures were expanded and differing views talked about. The substance of most of the points which arose in this way is given in the seminar notes printed after the main text. For those who do not wish to plough through these detailed notes I have appended a short list of books for further reading. The lectures were illustrated with lantern slides and some of these illustrations are printed here in the plates: their intention is to illustrate the variety of person and performance among the first seven civilizations of man. And let me emphasize, the theme throughout is not the content and development of these civilizations, but the light archaeology throws on their origins and interrelations and therefore on the general process of synoecism.

In the preparation of this book I have been very glad to be able to continue the co-operation with Mr H. A. Shelley which has gone on for the last few years in the pages of *Antiquity* and many volumes in the *Ancient Peoples and Places* series, and thank him for the fourteen maps he has drawn for me.

St John's College,   G.D.
Cambridge,
May 1968

CHAPTER ONE

SAVAGERY, BARBARISM
AND CIVILIZATION

IN a recent article in the *Spectator*, Professor Stuart Piggott referred to archaeology as 'the science of rubbish'.[1] He was indicating that archaeology is the study of what material has been left behind, of the minor monuments that time 'which antiquates antiquities, and hath an art to make dust of all things, hath yet spared', of the dead bones which have 'quietly rested under the drums and tramplings of three conquests', to quote Sir Thomas Browne. Do you also remember Francis Bacon's definition of what archaeology was concerned with? 'Antiquities,' he said, 'are history defaced or some remnants of history which have casually escaped the shipwreck of time.'[2]

It is with these remnants of history, this rubbish that has escaped the shipwreck of time, that this book is concerned. When I saw the title of Professor Piggott's article I was immediately reminded of the fine condemnation of archaeology once uttered by that most amusing American professor of anthropology, the late Ernest Alfred Hooton. 'Archaeology,' he said, 'implies an interest in the obsolete paraphernalia of the past, which to the multitude stigmatizes its students as unregardful of the necessities of the present – the senile playboys of science rooting in the rubbish heaps of antiquity.'[3] I am one of these senile playboys and I am asking you to root in the rubbish heaps of antiquity with me: let us dig archaeology together to find what light it throws on what I regard as one of the most important historical problems – the problem of the beginnings of the ancient civilization of man. Our theme, then, is what archaeology, the study of the material remains of the human past, tells us about the origin of the civilized societies of antiquity, about the origin of the earliest and first civilized societies – that is to say about the origins of civilization itself.[4]

This is a large theme and I shall of course do no more than touch on some of the most important and significant aspects of this problem. But I do not shirk this task, because I believe that from time to time this great problem should be discussed in a general way, and that professional archaeologists should from time to time stop looking at their particular tree – in my case the megalithic monuments of western Europe – and look at the wood.[5] The first book that studied the origins of civilization from evidence of archaeology was published almost a hundred years ago: it was called *The Origins of Civilization*. It was written by the banker, politician, scholar, Member of Parliament who was born to the name John Lubbock, became Sir John Lubbock, Bart, and was raised to the peerage as Lord Avebury – someone said cynically at the time of his elevation: 'And how long shall we have to wait until he becomes Viscount Stonehenge?' We owe many things to Lubbock – the beginning of our Ancient Monuments Inspectorate, and Bank Holidays, which were for a short while called Sir John Lubbock's Days. It was he who introduced into common English parlance the words prehistory and prehistoric, and coined the neo-Graecisms, Palaeolithic and Neolithic. This he did in his book *Prehistoric Times*, first published just over a hundred years ago, in 1865. Incidentally, copies of its seventh edition were still for sale in Heffers and Bowes and Bowes when I came up to Cambridge as an undergraduate more than thirty years ago.[6]

Lubbock's *The Origins of Civilization* came out five years after his *Prehistoric Times*. It was the work of an archaeologist and natural scientist studying a problem for which the sources were part material, that is to say, archaeological; and part literary, that is to say, historical in the narrow sense of written history, history *sensu stricto*. We realize today that written sources can tell us next to nothing about the origins of the first civilized societies: the problem is an archaeological one. Many – too many – who have written about the origins of civilization since Lubbock's time have failed to appreciate this fact: the literature abounds in geographical, historical and philosophical generalizations. Here we have little use for these: the problem is archaeological, and our concern is with the hard facts of archaeology.

A notable and modern example of a distinguished historian who attacked this problem of the origins of civilization without appreciating the role of archaeology is Professor Arnold Toynbee. His, admittedly monumental, *A Study of History*, markedly neglects the evidence of the monuments of history, notably the minor monuments which 'time hath spared', the artifacts of the preliterate people from which prehistory is written. Toynbee is a classic example of the truth that a historian cannot live by written sources alone.[7] This is not a personal view or a private prejudice; it is, I think, the view of most people who study the very ancient past of man, whether the sources are material or literary. Let me quote the views of Dr Ignacio Bernal, of the Escuela Nacional de Antropología of Mexico and Director of the National Museum of Anthropology, Mexico. Speaking in 1963 at the end of a symposium on prehistoric man in America he said:

I once attempted to explore the usefulness of applying Toynbee's ideas on the birth, growth and death of civilizations to the known facts of Mesoamerican archaeology. It became evident that nearly all his factual data are inaccurate, incomplete, and badly outdated. I tried to show that his ideas could nevertheless be applied usefully to Mesoamerican development and that they constitute at least one mode of interpretation, offering a plausible explanation of the 'why' of civilization, as well as the 'how'. . . . My efforts were received with a sad smile, which seemed to say, we live in a free world and every man is entitled to a little foolishness.[8]

Until Lubbock's time man's history was conventionally divided into modern, medieval and ancient. Lubbock defined the fourth division, that of prehistory – a kind of misnomer: it really means pre-written history. Writing is an achievement which came late in man's cultural development: the earliest surviving writing comes from Egypt and Mesopotamia and is not earlier than about 3000 B.C.[9] Writing, then, is a skill which is some five thousand years old. Man may have come into existence, perhaps in Africa, one to one and a half million years ago. *Homo sapiens* was certainly in existence thirty to forty thousand years ago, and possibly much earlier. At a very conservative estimate the pre-literate, prehistoric past of *homo sapiens* is ten times as long as written history, and the prehistoric past of man as a genus *Homo* very much longer. It is the final stages of the long pre-literate past that concern us here, and it is the testimony of the spade, and not the testimony of the written word, that suggests to us the views we should now take about the origins of civilized societies. By the time writing has arrived and recorded history is upon us, civilized societies have already been born.[10]

There is a difficulty here, a difficulty of method and approach. The historian proper is suspicious of the historian improper, if I may so call the archaeologist who copes with the science of prehistoric 'rubbish', the scholar who deals with pots and pans and ruins, and invents names for the people who created non-literate cultures. And on his side the archaeologist is suspicious of the broad approaches made by the historian and philosopher of history and often retreats to his taxonomy and typology and takes refuge in the minu·tiae of ancient material culture. This is why the problem we are studying here is so fascinating and so fraught with dangers and pitfalls, for it needs archaeological knowledge and a breadth of historical thinking. We may not achieve the union of these, but let us try.

Our picture of man's remote past is derived from archaeology, with all its associated scientific disciplines such as, for example, human palaeontology, geochronology, and the study of faunal and floral remains. The relative values of the material and literary sources for reconstructing the past of man vary from the beginnings to the present day. In pre-history, as we have said, archaeology is paramount; indeed prehistory *is* prehistoric archaeology. In ancient history archaeology is of very great importance, and sometimes much of it is referred to as proto-history. We cannot solve or begin to see our way towards a solution of the fascinating problem of man's emergence from savagery through illiterate barbarism to literate civilization until and unless we appreciate what archaeology has to say; how much it has to say, and sometimes how little – we will speak of the limitations of archaeology later. The limitations of the written sources, on the other hand, are more obvious: they just do not exist before 3000 B.C. in the Near East. The antiquity of man's first civilizations is buried in the pre-literate past and it is what archaeology tells about the last stages of that pre-literate past as it emerges via proto-history into history that is our concern.[11]

The word 'civilization' is by no means a very old one in the English language. Boswell reports that in 1772 he urged Dr Johnson to insert the word in his Dictionary, but the Doctor declined: he preferred the older word 'civility', and this, like the word 'urbanity', reflected the culture of the townsman in *urbs* or *civitas* as distinct from that of the barbarian – the agricultural rustic. It was of course an invidious term: here we use civilization and urbanization as objective and specific terms – terms without the overtones which we associate with the words civility and urbanity. We do not suggest that the people of the first civilizations, the literate town-dwellers of Ur and Mohenjo-daro and Anyang, were necessarily civil or urbane. But they were literate and lived in towns and were the first people to do so in the long process of man's cultural and social evolution from the darkest savagery of the early Palaeolithic.

I have already used the words culture and civilization several times: the best way to define them is to quote what the late Professor A. L. Kroeber said. Kroeber (1876–1960) was one of the great pioneer American anthropologists. From 1957 onwards he began to set down in outline material for a book he never finished: it was called *A Roster of Civilizations and Culture*, and this is what he wrote on a sheet found after his death in his files for this book:

The terms civilization and culture are used here not contrastively and exclusively, but inclusively as essential synonyms of sometimes varying accent. There is no difference of principle between the two words, they denote somewhat distinguishable grades of degree of the same thing. Civilization currently carries an overtone of high development of a society: culture has become the customary term of universal denotation in this range, applicable alike to high or low products and heritages of socie-

ties. Every human society has its culture, complex or simple ...
for the larger and richer cultures the term civilization has current usage, and need not be quarrelled with, on the understanding that no distinctions of kind between civilization and culture
are implied.[12]

In my view this definition cannot be bettered for clearness
and correctness. There are no implied distinctions of kind
or value involved. I might add just one thing to make clearer
the difference between the archaeological/anthropological
use of the words culture and civilization, and the ordinary
descriptive use of these words with value-judgements. All
men by definition have culture, but all men by practice are
not necessarily cultivated. Most men these days belong in
whole or in part to a civilization – that is to say to a particular
pattern of culture – but many others, the so-called primi-
tives, still live in a society that has not attained to this complexity. And all men who are part of a civilization are not
necessarily civilized or civil.[13]

Lubbock, though he was an archaeologist – among many
other things – was writing at a time before many of the great
archaeological discoveries of man's earliest civilizations had
been made. He wrote, too, at a time when, though Charles
Darwin had disturbed complacent people by the publication
of his *The Origin of Species* in 1859, and Charles Lyell and
John Evans had further disturbed people by their accept-
ance, in that very same *annus mirabilis*, of the great antiquity of man, there was a fairly clear and a fairly comfortable
idea as to what civilization was. It was Western Europe,
and the Victorian age was the proud pinnacle of that edifice,
Western Civilization. We all of us, in a wide variety of ways,
still use this tag phrase, Western Civilization. We are proud
of it, ashamed of it, it is the great glory of democracy and
Christianity, it is bourgeois capitalism, we are ready to die

for it, it is effete and already dying on its feet: it all depends on how you look at it. And in many a place we still encounter the traditional history-book picture of the evolution and the components of Western Civilization – the three components from Athens and Rome and Jerusalem. Athens gave Western Civilization its intellectual and artistic heritage, Rome the practical achievement of government and law, and Jerusalem its faith and morals. Viewed thus it is all as simple as that, and the notion is often repeated in this simplistic form.

But even in the nineteenth century this over-simple story of the three civilizations which lay behind the medieval and modern West – Greek, Roman and Hebrew – was obviously not a complete and full story. The humanist and the Christian, even without detailed archaeological sources, and relying on the dubious historicity of the Bible, and the more accurate observations and descriptions of men like Herodotus, knew of Egyptians and Assyrians and Babylonians, and of Medes and Persians. Most scholars had forgotten, or had chosen to forget, that in the period between 1492 and 1530, the period from Columbus to Amerigo Vespucci, civilizations had been discovered and in part destroyed by the Spanish conquistadors in Central America. It is, incidentally, one of the curiosities of the development of the study of man's antiquity in the British Isles that we have hitherto paid very little attention to the pre-Columbian civilizations of America. The average cultivated reader probably knows even less about the Maya, the Aztecs and the Incas of America than he does about the ancient Egyptians, the Sumerians, the Harappans and the people of the Shang civilization of China.[14]

But if the Victorians thought little about what lay behind Greece and Rome and the Medes and the Persians, and paid little attention to Central America, they had some vague ideas of the antiquity of civilized life in India and China. Had not China invented paper and gunpowder, and were there not sahibs and *quai hais* who had seen some damned interesting old remains in the jungles of India, and was there not among a few a feeling that, rope-tricks and sword-swallowing fakirs apart, there was some very ancient wisdom in the East? We were in the nineteenth century and many of us still are occidentocentric. As the late Professor Ralph Linton said in *The Tree of Culture*, itself a very valuable introduction to the cultural evolution of man, 'It has been said that the battle of Waterloo was won on the playing fields of Eton, and one might add that Singapore was lost in its classrooms.'[15]

The revolution through archaeology in our knowledge of man's earliest civilizations took place in the seventy-five years that succeeded *The Origin of Species* and Lubbock's *Prehistoric Times*. In 1877 Ernest de Sarzec, the French consul at Basra, began digging at a place called Telloh, where stone statuettes had been found; and, during the next quarter century, he found the Sumerians through archaeology. In 1871 Heinrich Schliemann began digging at Hissarlik in western Turkey and found Troy. On and off he dug until his death in 1890, and in between his four archaeological campaigns in Troy, he excavated at Mycenae and Tiryns and revealed to the world a new civilization, that of the Mycenaeans. Schliemann was negotiating for permission to dig in Crete when he died: in 1899 Arthur Evans began excavations at Knossos, and in nine weeks uncovered a vast building which he identified as the palace of Minos. The next year he announced the existence of an early civilization which he labelled the Minoan.[16]

In the first volume of *The Cambridge History of India*

Figure 1. Locations of the first civilizations

which was published in 1922, Sir John Marshall wrote: 'It is the misfortune of Indian history that its earliest and most obscure pages derive little light from contemporary antiquities.'[17] Two years later, in 1924, in the *Illustrated London News* he was announcing that excavations at Mohenjo-daro and Harappa, in what is now Pakistan, had revealed a new prehistoric civilization, that now usually referred to as the Indus or Harappan civilization. During the last few decades of the nineteenth century farmers tilling their fields near Anyang in north China found curious bits of decorated bones, the so-called oracle-bones. In 1928 the Academica Sinica and the Smithsonian Institution began to dig at

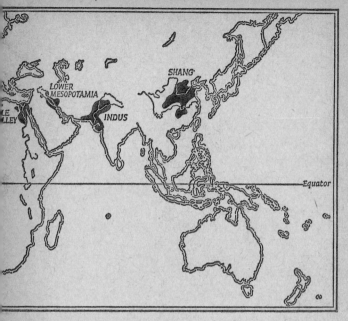

Anyang and revealed the prehistoric Bronze Age civilization of China, now firmly identified with the Shang dynasty
of the Chinese historians.[18]

And from China to Peru. The last thirty to forty years of
reconnaissance and excavation in Middle America and Peru
have revealed the origin and growth of the nuclear American
civilizations. So that we are now in a very different position
from Lubbock's when he set out to write his *Origins of
Civilization* in 1870. We now believe that we know from
archaeology the whereabouts and the whenabouts of the first
civilizations of man – in southern Mesopotamia, in Egypt,
in the Indus Valley, in the Yellow River in China, in the

Valley of Mexico, in the jungles of Guatemala and Honduras and the coastlands and highlands of Peru. In these seven areas the first civilizations came into existence. We will not call them primary civilizations because this makes it difficult to refer to Crete, Mycenae, the Hittites, and Greece and Rome as other than secondary civilizations, and this term 'secondary' seems to have a pejorative meaning. We shall talk rather of the first, the earliest civilizations, and of later civilizations.[19]

Let us go back for a moment to the central question of what is civilization: we answered it immediately by quoting from Kroeber – let us begin again. The *Oxford English Dictionary* defines civilization as 'the action or process of ... being civilized', or 'the state or condition of being civilized'. This itself begs a question which is answered when we look up the definition of 'to civilize'. There we are told that it means 'to bring out of a state of barbarism, to instruct in the arts of life, to enlighten and refine.' Taking the *Oxford English Dictionary* as an accurate mirror of current English usage, as, being a Cambridge man, I always do, civilization is seen as the process of changing what Addison called 'the rude unpolish'd world' into a civilized, polished world. We are not as extravagant as Somerset Maugham who said: 'The degree of a nation's civilization is marked by its disregard for the necessities of existence.'

Kroeber's definition was that civilization was a particular pattern of culture. Gordon Childe, in his books *Man Makes Himself* and *What Happened in History*, listed the elements which he thought made up the pattern of the urban civilized communities of the ancient Near East – the plough, the wheeled cart, traction animals, the sailing boat, the smelting of copper ores, the solar calendar, writing, processes of reckoning, standards of measurement, irrigation, specialized craftsmen, city-life, a surplus of foodstuffs available to support those members of the community who are no longer themselves producing their own food. Certainly the common features in the subsistence of the early civilizations are these: first, the existence of a surplus from the soil to meet and support new economic classes; second, a complex subsistence pattern – not one based on a single crop – and some degree of intensive land use of which irrigation was one technique. Childe's list is mainly one of material things. Redfield, in his analysis of civilization, stresses in addition four things: one, the value placed upon the central accumulation of capital collected through tribute or taxation; two, special privileges to the ruling class; three, the high value accorded to 'the State'; four, the rise of national religions, priestly classes, god-rulers or god-priests and ceremonial-bureaucratic centres.[20]

In 1958 the Oriental Institute of the University of Chicago held a symposium on the origins of civilization in the Near East: the papers prepared for the symposium and the lectures and discussions that took place were published in 1960 in a book entitled *City Invincible*. Quite naturally, many who took part in this invaluable symposium produced their own definitions of civilization. The late Professor Clyde Kluckhohn said that a society to be called civilized must have two of the following: towns upward of 5,000 people, a written language, and monumental ceremonial centres. Gelb argued that you could not have civilization without writing. 'I have reached the conclusion,' he said, 'that writing is of such importance that civilization cannot exist without it, and, conversely, that writing cannot exist except in a civilization.' Professor Robert Adams's definition of a civilization was a society with a functionally interrelated set of social institutions which he listed as:

31

1. class stratification marked by highly different degrees of ownership of control of the main productive resources;
2. Political and religious hierarchies complementing each other in the administration of territorially organized states; and
3. complex division of labour with full-time craftsmen, servants, soldiers and officials alongside the great mass of primary peasant producers.[21]

One other definition, this time not from the Chicago conference, but by Professor Stuart Piggott, from his Preface to Professor Max Mallowan's recently published *Early Mesopotamia and Iran*:

We should surely not be far from the mark if we thought of civilized societies as those which worked out a solution to the problem of living in a relatively permanent community, at a level of technological and societal development above that of the hunting band, the family farmstead, the rustic self-sufficient village or the pastoral tribe, and with a capacity for storing information in the form of written documents or their equivalent. Civilization, like all human culture at whatsoever level, is something artificial and man-made, the result of making tools (physical and conceptual) of increasing complexity in response to the enlarging concepts of community life developing in men's minds.[22]

When we speak, then, of the origins of civilization we mean the origins of the first literate town-dwellers; we are discussing what Gordon Childe called the Urban Revolution – but we shall see that what I prefer to call the process of synoecism was not a revolution but an evolution, and one that took place in several parts of the world. Our problem is how and why and where and when barbarian societies made this leap forward into literate town-dwelling communities. And here is the nub of the question: did this forward leap take place once only, or did it take place many times? Before we are equipped to answer this question, or even to discuss the relative merits of the various answers that have been given from time to time, we must go through the archaeological evidence in the crucial areas. First we will discuss Mesopotamia, then Egypt, then India and China, and finally the archaeological evidence from America.

We have already begged another question by referring over and over again to barbarism. The Greeks knew what they meant by barbarians: they called them *barbaroi* which is the same thing as *barbarophonoi*, that is to say the people who spoke a foreign or barbarian language – the people who went '*Bar! bar!*' The Greeks met these people on the frontiers of the civilized world and had names for them such as Sarmatians and Scythians and Celts and Ligurians. Herodotus gave an account of a people living in a lake village in Greece, and here he was writing an ethnographical account of what we nowadays would call a Neolithic or Bronze Age community.[23] The barbarians whom the Greeks met had many things in common – they were illiterate, they didn't live in towns, some of them were nomadic and drank mare's milk, and some of them, surprisingly, wore trousers. But their worst crime was that they didn't speak Greek – and that showed clearly how barbarian they were!

Yet the barbarians, although they had no towns or writing or literature, were accomplished in many arts and crafts. They had domesticated animals – indeed many of them were horse-riders – and they cultivated grain. Some of them, like the Celts and Scythians, had developed a remarkable style of art.[24] They were indeed near-civilized, or so thought the Greeks.

The Greeks did not often meet people who were not

agriculturists or herders; they did not have many dealings with those human beings whom from the Middle Ages onwards we have been calling savages: *silvaticus* from *silva* a wood or forest. Savages were the people of the woods and forests – the uncultivated ones, and they certainly did not know the cultivation of grains: even in 1588 the word was being used for uncivilized people living in the lowest state of culture – people in a state of nature: and you may remember Tennyson's phrase: 'I will take some savage woman, she shall rear my dusky race.'[25]

By the late eighteenth century there was a clear awareness, among some scholars at least, of savages, barbarians and civilized people as the three stages in man's social and cultural evolution. Governor Pownall – he was Governor of Massachusetts – wrote in Volume II of *Archaeologia* in 1773:

This globe of earth hath, according to the process of its nature, existed under a successive change of forms, and been inhabited by various species of mankind, living under various modes of life, suited to that particular state of the earth in which they existed. The face of the earth being originally everywhere covered with wood, except where water prevailed, the first human beings of it were *Woodland-Men* living on the fruits, fish and game of the forest. To these the land-worker succeeded. He *settled* on the land, became a fixed inhabitant and increased and multiplied. Where-ever the land-worker came, he, as at this day, ate out the scattered race of Wood-men.[26]

In the late eighteenth century there was speculation about the succession: Woodland-men, the men of *silva*, the salvages or savages; then the Land-Workers – the settled people, the barbarians of the Greeks – and finally, civilization. This was the threefold sequence of food-gatherers, primitive agriculturists and herders, civilization; in a word, or rather in three words – Savagery, Barbarism, and Civilization. Sven Nilsson, Professor of Zoology at Lund University in Sweden, set out these views in his *Skandinaviska Nordens Urinvanåre*, the first edition of which was published in Lund in 1838–43. The second edition was translated into English – actually by John Lubbock – and appeared in 1868 under the title of *The Primitive Inhabitants of Scandinavia*. Here Nilsson sets out a classification of man's past based on the mode of subsistence. First there was the *savage* state – the childhood of the race – when man was a hunter, fisher and collector of berries and fruits. Secondly, the *herdsman* or *nomad* stage, when hunting was an occasional occupation but man subsisted mainly on the products of his herds. The third stage was the *agricultural*, and the fourth *civilization*, which, incidentally, Nilsson defined on the basis of coined money, writing and the division of labour. His idea of a herding or pastoral stage between food-gathering and agriculture lingered on long, and it is rather curious to find the poet Coleridge saying in 1836 that 'the progress from savagery to civilization is evidently first from the hunting to the pastoral stage.'

The anthropologists and ethnographers of the nineteenth century who were beginning to interest the world in existing primitive societies and the fascinating problems of their inter-relationships with the past of modern societies – was it progress and development or retrogression and decay? – did not necessarily accept the four-stage model of Nilsson, namely, savage food-gatherer, herdsman-nomad, agriculturist and civilized man, but they did accept in general the model of savagery, barbarism and civilization, and this has been with us ever since. I have no complaint about it in its thoroughly general way. Its first clear formal statement was in Edward Tylor's *Anthropology: An Introduction to the*

Study of Man and Civilization, published in 1881. Tylor became the first Reader in Anthropology in Britain, and then the first Professor, at Oxford, which was, for once, on the side of the winning causes. Tylor proposed formally to distinguish three stages in human history: savagery; barbarism, which he defined as beginning with agriculture; and civilization, which he began with writing.[27]

The American anthropologist Lewis H. Morgan, in his *Ancient Society: or Researches in the Lines of Human Progress from Savagery through Barbarism to Civilization* (1877), proceeded to define these terms more exactly according to the enlargement of man's sources of subsistence. He distinguished seven periods – seven ethnic periods as he called them. The first six were:

1. *Lower Savagery*, from the emergence of man to the discovery of fire;
2. *Middle Savagery*, from the discovery of fire to the discovery of the bow and arrow;
3. *Upper Savagery*, from the discovery of the bow and arrow to the discovery of pottery;
4. *Lower Barbarism*. This stage began with the discovery of pottery (which, to Morgan, was the dividing line between Savagery and Barbarism) and ended with the domestication of animals;
5. *Middle Barbarism*, from the domestication of animals to the smelting of iron ore;
6. *Upper Barbarism*, from the discovery of iron to the invention of the phonetic alphabet.

Finally, the seventh period was civilization with writing and the alphabet.[28]

These schemes of Tylor and Morgan were of course

theoretical ones; they were models of the past like the sim-
pler models of Pownall and Nilsson. At the same time as
Nilsson was writing, another model was being developed,
mainly in Denmark: it was a technological model and saw
man's past in three stages or ages of Stone, Bronze and Iron.
C. J. Thomsen, the first Curator of the Danish National
Museum at Copenhagen, opened this museum to the public
in 1819 with its exhibits classified in this way. His assistant
and eventual successor, J. J. A. Worsaae, demonstrated that
these three successive technologies were not merely a theoretical model, but were the proven and observed fact of
excavations. It was the great contribution of Worsaae to
show in his digging in the Danish peat bogs and the bar-
rows of Jutland that man had once lived in a stone age, and
then had become metal-using, but only knew copper and its
alloy with tin, namely bronze; and that only late in his
evolution – we know now that it was not before 1500 B.C.
in Anatolia and much later in other parts of the world,
500 B.C. in this country – man became iron-using.[29]

It was soon realized that there were several stages of the
Stone Age, and it was Lubbock, a hundred years ago, who
produced the terms 'Palaeolithic' and 'Neolithic' for the
Old and New Stone Ages. A Mesolithic was added later,
and by some an Eolithic, and all the five ages – Palaeolithic,
Mesolithic, Neolithic, Bronze Age and Iron Age – were
divided into epochs and periods reflecting in their turn
various patterns of material culture and various groupings
of artifacts.

Two people at least tried to marry together the two
models. One was the late Gordon Childe, the other J. G. D.
Clark, at present Disney Professor of Archaeology in Cambridge. If you look at Childe's classic *What Happened in
History*, first published in 1942, you will find chapters

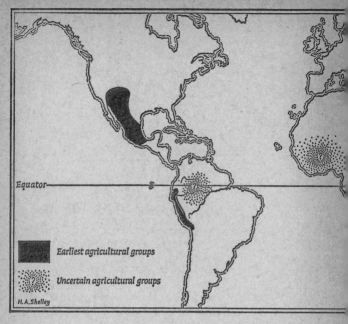

Equator

Earliest agricultural groups

Uncertain agricultural groups

H. A. Shelley

Figure 2. Locations of the earliest agricultural communities

labelled Palaeolithic Savagery, Neolithic Barbarism, the Higher Barbarism of the Copper Age, Early Bronze Age Civilization, and so on. To me these marriages of the two models are not very helpful; indeed, as I have myself been advocating for years, the technological model, which served us so well for so long – and without which perhaps archaeology would never have developed as a discipline – can now happily be abandoned in general parlance, though it will for long be used taxonomically, and we shall all see on museum labels for the rest of our days tags like Upper Palaeolithic, Middle Neolithic and so on.[30]

It is, incidentally, particularly interesting that in the de-

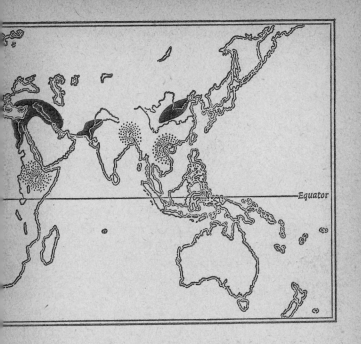

Equator

velopment of pre-Columbian American archaeology which will be our concern later, we shall find that after a period of using the old neo-Graecist labels, American archaeology has devised a terminology of its own, with phrases like Lithic, Archaic, Formative, Classic and post-Classic. We shall discuss these later: I do not find them entirely satisfactory, but they are certainly very useful constructs. The Classic phase is the phase of early American civilization in Mexico, Yucatán and Peru.[31]

You may well ask why this is a suitable moment for rediscussing the whole problem of the origins of that special pattern of culture which we have agreed to label civilization: what has happened, if you like to put it this way, since the last war to bring these wide issues again to the forefront? My answer to this is threefold: first, there have been new excavations and new discoveries of far-reaching kinds – the discovery of Eridu in Mesopotamia, for example, claimed, and surely correctly, as the oldest of all cities; the re-excavation of Mohenjo-daro and Harappa with the fresh light it has thrown on these Indus cities; the discovery of many new Indus sites; the excavations in China which have taken us back to the origins of the Shang civilization; and then, endless work in Mesoamerica and Peru culminating in the discovery of the origins of American agriculture.

First then, discovery, fresh facts. But secondly, the dating of these facts. It has always been difficult and often defeating to find accurate dates for events before the invention of writing in Mesopotamia five thousand years ago; and dates for barbarian cultures and civilizations that were completely outside the range of contact with the early chronologies of the ancient Near East. Archaeology has for long badly needed a technique of dating independent of man and writing. The first geochronological techniques were dendrochronology, developed in America and able to take pre-Columbian American cultures back fifteen hundred years before Columbus, to about the time of the birth of Christ; and geochronology in the narrow sense of the word, that is to say, counting of clay varves – the thin layer of clay left behind by the melt waters of the retreating glaciers – which enabled the Swedish geologist Baron de Geer to calculate a date for the end of the last Ice Age and to provide a geochronology of the last twelve thousand years. The inter-relation of the study of pollens with the dated clay varves has brought about a tremendous extension of geochronology and the provision of a time-table of the post-glacial vegetational and climatic phases.[32]

But the great breakthrough, perhaps the greatest breakthrough in the development of archaeology, came as a result of research in nuclear physics in the last war. Professor Willard F. Libby, then Professor of Physics in Chicago and now Professor of Chemistry in California – the first Nobel prizeman in archaeology, as he has been described – discovered that it was possible to date absolutely organic objects from the past, such as bone and charcoal, because when an organism died its Carbon 12 content remained constant but its Carbon 14 content disintegrated at a fixed rate. There are now over seventy laboratories all over the world engaged in producing these radiocarbon dates.[33]

It is because of this revolutionary geochronological technique that we can now state as historical facts that:

1. The savages of the Upper Palaeolithic in southern France and northern Spain who lived by hunting and fishing and collecting fruit and berries, whose cultures have names like Aurignacian, Solutrean and Magdalenian, and who produced the cave art of Lascaux, Niaux and Altamira, lived from around about 35,000 to 10,000 B.C.;[34]
2. The beginnings of the domestication of animals and the cultivation of grain first took place in the ancient Near East about ten thousand years ago. The great American orientalist James Breasted invented the phrase 'the Fertile Crescent' for the grassland hill-slopes that existed from Egypt through Palestine to northern Mesopotamia and western Iran, and it is here that, as he guessed, the first farmers came into existence. This was a region which had wild wheat and barley and wild sheep and goats. Our first farmers occur in northern Mesopotamia and Palestine but also in a third

area outside the Fertile Crescent of Breasted – in southern Anatolia;[35]

3. Civilization, in the sense in which we are using the word, did not develop in the foothills of the Zagros Mountains or in Palestine or in southern Anatolia – did not in fact develop in the Fertile Crescent or where the first peasant farmers flourished. It developed in southern Mesopotamia and the next two chapters will deal with this. Professor Samuel Kramer wrote a book about early Mesopotamia called *History begins at Sumer* – a fine, catchpenny title, but also true; man did first achieve civilization on the flood plains of the twin rivers, the Tigris and Euphrates.

We think of this problem anew in the first place because we now have new facts and the facts are soundly dated. We may guess at origins and interrelations, but we no longer have to, or are allowed to, guess at dates. New facts, accurate dates; but there is a third reason why the present moment is opportune for a re-discussion of the general issues involved – a change in the climate of archaeological thought. There used to be a great dispute in all archaeological and anthropological circles, the dispute between diffusion and independent invention or evolution, in which the protagonists of diffusion went sometimes to great extremes, in their hyperdiffusionism, deriving all civilization, all the higher arts, from one place, usually Egypt or Sumer. In the last twenty-five years or so we have lived in a climate of thought which is a kind of modified diffusionism. A very good example of this is Gordon Childe's *What Happened in History*, a book that has coloured the thinking of most people up to the present day.

Now it appears to some of us that Childe did not give sufficient attention to the possibilities of independent invention and of parallel development. I have already referred to E. B. Tylor's *Anthropology*; in another book, *Researches into the Early History of Mankind* (1865), he said: 'Civilization, being a process of long and complex growth, can only be thoroughly understood when studied throughout its entire range. . . . Sometimes it may be ascribed to the like working of men's minds under like conditions, and sometimes, it is a proof of blood relationship, or of intercourse, direct or indirect, between the races among whom it is found.' These wise words were written a hundred years ago, and I think we will find ourselves largely in agreement with them when we have examined the new facts and new dates of whose existence Tylor could never have dreamt.[36]

Robert Lowie, in his *History of Ethnological Theory*, described moments in the nineteenth century when 'Evolution . . . lay down amicably beside Diffusion',[37] and surely it still may. Man, the civilized animal, is the product partly of independent and parallel development among the first peasant village communities of the Old and New Worlds, and partly the product of the cross-fertilization of ideas and peoples between the oldest civilized societies which we will be discussing in the next six chapters. We shall return to the general theory of cultural origins in the last chapter.

CHAPTER TWO

THE DISCOVERY OF THE
FIRST CIVILIZATION

In the eleventh chapter of *Genesis* are these words:

And it came to pass, as they journeyed from the east, that they found a plain in the land of Shinar, and they dwelt there.

And they said to one another, Go to, let us make brick, and burn them throughly. And they had brick for stone, and slime had they for morter.

And they said, Go to, let us build us a city and a tower, whose top may reach unto heaven; and let us make us a name, lest we be scattered abroad upon the face of the whole earth.

These words were set down in Hebrew not earlier than 800 B.C. and give, in a few sentences, an account of the origins of the earliest, the oldest, the first civilization made by man – the civilization of the land of Shinar, the land of Sumer. They did make a name for themselves, and that name was the Sumerians.[38]

In this and the next chapter our concern is with the light which archaeology throws on the origins of Sumerian civilization. I have already referred to the doubtful historicity of the Bible, and by that I meant our inability to accept all that is in the beginning of the Old Testament as a true and certain guide to the origin of the world, the genesis of man and the development of his culture from the savagery – if that is the right word – of the Garden of Eden through the peasant agriculture of Cain and the stock-raising of Abel to the city life of Babel and to the ancient civilizations of the Near East which the Old Testament people witnessed in

Egypt, Babylon and elsewhere. But, hidden in that interesting congeries of myths and legends, many directly derived from Mesopotamia before Abraham set off from Ur of the Chaldees, are some historical facts, as we shall see, and indeed as it is easy to see nowadays with the hindsight of a hundred and more years of archaeological research in southwest Asia. Noah and the Flood must surely reflect some of the floods that inundated lower Mesopotamia from time to time, and did flood the known world though not of course the whole world; and the story of the conflict between Abel and Cain is a reflection of the conflict between the steppe and the sown, the desert and the irrigated river valley – a constant theme in ancient Mesopotamian history.[39]

Sumer is the territory which after 2000 B.C. was called Babylonia. The plain of the land of Shinar is the land between the rivers, the land between the twin rivers, the Tigris and the Euphrates. The Greeks called this land Mesopotamia, which word means just that – the land between the rivers. Most of it today is part of the modern state of Iraq although the Euphrates rises in Syria and the Tigris in Turkey. From the Turkish border and the Armenian mountains in the north to the Persian Gulf in the south is roughly six hundred miles, about the distance from Aberdeen to Dover. From the Syrian Desert on the west to the mountains of Persia – the Zagros Mountains – on the east is some two hundred to two hundred and fifty miles. In this area, and more especially in the south, the Sumerian civilization came into existence in the second half of the fourth millennium B.C.[40]

That Mesopotamia had been the homeland of ancient civilizations was of course very well known for a long time. Babylon and Assyria were part of the historical picture of man based on classical writers and the Old Testament.

Herodotus visited Babylon in 450 B.C. and described the great temple or *ziggurat* there [Plates 1–3]; he said that 'as a grain-bearing country Assyria is the richest in the world.' The figures given by Strabo and Herodotus for a yield of corn of two to three hundredfold may not have been wildly exaggerated. Jacobsen has calculated from the cuneiform texts that the yield of wheat in southern Iraq in 2400 B.C. could compare favourably with that of the best modern Canadian wheatfields, and this may well be one of the reasons for the growth and the flourishing of Sumerian civilization – for fertility and agricultural wealth of southern Mesopotamia – when well farmed. I should of course have said 'pre-disposing conditions' rather than 'reasons': I do not want here or at any other point in this book to appear to slip into an easy economic or geographical determinism.

The Jews had been captive in Babylon and by its waters had wept. Everyone knows the dramatic account of the Hebrew poet-prophet Daniel who was an unwilling guest at Belshazzar's feast: 'Belshazzar the king made a great feast to a thousand of his lords, and drank wine before the thousand.' During the feast Cyrus's men waded across the river and broke into the city: 'In the same hour came forth fingers of a man's hand, and wrote ... upon the plaister of the wall of the king's palace ... and this writing was written, *Mene, mene, tekel, upharsin.*' This was in 538 B.C. The Babylonians and Assyrians had ruled in Mesopotamia off and on since 2000 B.C. Hammurabi was the greatest of the Babylonian kings and the author of the famous Code of Law issued by him

> To cause justice to prevail in the country,
> To destroy the wicked and evil,
> That the strong may not oppress the weak.

Hammurabi's dates have long been a matter for discussion: Professor Sydney Smith argued for a long chronology and his argument which gave the date of Hammurabi's accession as 1792 B.C. has been much strengthened by recent evidence.

You may well ask who were the Chaldeans and what exactly was Chaldea in this study of ancient peoples and early civilizations. Most people have heard of Abraham as living in 'Ur of the Chaldees' (*Genesis*, xi, 28); the terms Chaldees, Chaldeans, Chaldea are frequent in the Old Testament where they are used as equivalents for Babylonia and the Babylonians. The old term was *mat Kaldu*. Possibly at one early stage the Chaldeans were a separate Semitic-speaking people, but soon in ancient history they were indistinguishable from the Semitic-speaking peoples of Babylon.

So, nowadays, when we speak of the ancient peoples of Mesopotamia, we speak of Assyrians and Babylonians rather than of Assyrians and Chaldeans. By the way, subsequently the word Chaldee was wrongly used for the Aramaic language itself, while in the *Book of Daniel*, in Herodotus, Strabo and Diodorus it means astrologers and astronomers: and the term lived on for a long time to mean 'wise men'.[41]

There are two special features which have for long been associated in the minds of historians and archaeologists with early Mesopotamia. The first is the presence of *tells*, and the second is cuneiform writing [Plate 5]. Both need some brief words of explanation here. The early houses and temples of ancient Mesopotamia were built of clay, either of *pisé* (cob), which is roughly piled-up earth, or of *adobe*, shapeless lumps of clay pressed together. Later, sun-dried bricks were used and, latest of all, kiln-fired bricks which were naturally more durable especially when joined together with bitumen. These kiln-fired bricks were costly and reserved for the construction of temples and palaces: the great majority of Mesopotamian buildings were of clay or mud-brick. Rain and natural usage wore these mud-clay structures down, and it has been estimated that the average time-span of a mud house in Mesopotamia would be about seventy-five years. New houses were built on the collapsed and scattered remains of the old houses and so, over the centuries, there began to accumulate a man-made mound, a hill built accidentally out of man's own material past. These artificial and steadily accumulating mounds of successive settlements are called *tells* in Mesopotamia – this is incidentally a pre-Islamic word – and have other local names in other parts of the Near East, such as *tepe* in northern Mesopotamia and Iran, *hüyük* in Turkey. Sometimes they are very high indeed, and some of them, like Erbil (old Arbela), and Kirkuk, are still lived in – or perhaps one should say lived on; they have been more or less continuously occupied from very early times to the present day – perhaps for six to eight thousand years.[42]

These man-made settlement mounds – *tells*, *tepes*, *hüyüks* – are a feature of the archaeology of Iran, Iraq, Palestine and Turkey; they also occur in southern Russia and in Bulgaria. They are not a feature of the surviving past of barbarian Western and North-Western Europe, nor indeed of Egypt, where, as we shall see, traces of early settlements are difficult to find. Indeed one American archaeologist working in Egypt, John Wilson, has called the early civilization of Egypt 'a civilization without cities'. But where *tells* do occur they are an obvious place for the antiquary and traveller interested in the past, and for the modern archaeologist with his trenches, *sondages*, and large-scale excavations. This is why accounts of excavations in the Near East are full of numbered levels like Uruk XVIII, Tepe Gawra XII (a), Ninevite III, and so on. You will not be concerned with the minutiae of excavation reports, which are the secondary form of archaeological knowledge – the past as it seems to the excavator, as distinct from the *tells* themselves – the past as it survived. Here we are concerned with the third level of archaeological scholarship – the past as it seems to us from a synthesis of excavators' reports, but if you should ever refer to these sources – the excavation reports – you must bear in mind the fact that some excavations are published with the levels numbered from the top downwards as they appeared in the work of excavation, and others numbered from the bottom upwards in historical succession. Thus at Al 'Ubaid and Nineveh period I is the oldest, but at Uruk and Tepe Gawra it is the latest.

For a very long time before they were excavated the ancient mounds of the Near East were recognized as the remains of early settlements. The two large *tells* near Hillah in Babylonia and near Mosul in Assyria were pointed to in Jewish and Arab tradition as the sites of Babylon and Nineveh; and these and other sites were visited by European travellers from the twelfth century onwards. These travellers often collected bricks and potsherds and fragments of tablets from these *tells*. An Italian nobleman, Pietro della Valle, who wrote a most entertaining account of his journey across Mesopotamia, brought back to Europe in 1625 some baked clay tablets 'on which were writing in certain unknown characters'. This was cuneiform writing – the oldest writing in the world. The Sumerians wrote on clay, with a stylus made of a reed or wood [Plate 4]. The first signs set down were pictographic – a kind of picture writing as used

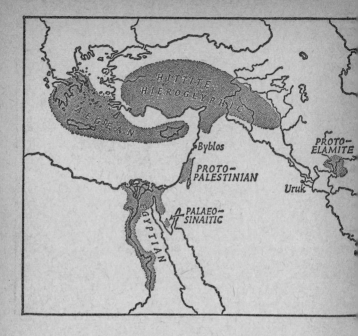

Figure 3. Distribution of non-cuneiform scripts in the Near Eastern Bronze Age [after Pope]

by the Chinese; later the Babylonians used the stylus for setting down a syllabic script. The cut edge of the reed stylus made wedge-shaped impressions, and hence the name cuneiform for this earliest writing.[43]

But it was not only on clay tablets that this cuneiform writing occurred. There were also monumental inscriptions. Faced with the writing on monuments and tablets, the learned world of Western Europe began to realize that here was a mystery, and a new field for scientific exploration. In 1761 the King of Denmark sent out a scientific ex-

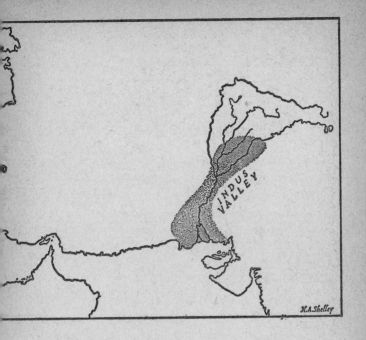

pedition to the east to gather as much information as possible in all fields, including archaeology. Its leader was Professor Karsten Niebuhr, a mathematician, but a man of very wide interests, who himself copied numerous inscriptions at Persepolis. Philologists began to work on the copies of these inscriptions. Niebuhr had himself noted that they seemed to be of three different kinds, and here he was right: they were in the three languages we now know to be Old Persian, Susian or Elamite, and Babylonian.

At the beginning of the nineteenth century, a young German by name Georg Friedrich Grotefend began working on Niebuhr's copyings of the Persepolis trilingual inscriptions.

In 1802, when only twenty-seven years of age, he had managed to decipher three royal names in the simplest of the three scripts, the old Persian, and later he managed to decipher correctly about a third of the letters in this language. By an inspired guess he had found the key to the decipherment of cuneiform writing. But, alas, Grotefend was not an oriental scholar; he was not a member of the Faculty of the University of Göttingen to whose Academy of Sciences he submitted a dissertation in Latin on his epoch-making discovery. Grotefend was a little-known college teacher and the Göttingen Academy, to their eternal shame, refused to publish his dissertation: it was in fact not published until 1893, when it was of purely historical interest, and by which time others had received the credit for the decipherment.[44]

From the sad story of Grotefend's rejection by the Göttingen Academy we pass to the success story of one of the most interesting and colourful characters in the development of Near Eastern studies – Henry Creswicke Rawlinson who lived from 1810 to 1895. He was a colonel in the Indian Army who got himself posted to Baghdad as British Resident and Consul-General; he was later knighted for his varied achievements. With a knowledge of oriental languages but no knowledge of Grotefend's work, he began to study the cuneiform inscriptions. He started on two short trilingual inscriptions from near Hamadan and then worked on the famous trilingual inscription [Plate 14] cut in 516 B.C. at the instruction of Darius Hystaspes (521–485 B.C.) on the great rock of Behistun or Bisotun, twenty-two miles east of Kermanshah. This inscription is cut four hundred feet above the ground on the face of a rock-mass which itself rises one thousand seven hundred feet from the plain. This giant inscription, 'a Mesopotamian Rosetta stone' as it has been called, measures 150 feet by 100. The difficulty lay in copying the inscription.

Rawlinson began working alone. In 1852 he wrote:

When I was living at Kermanshah fifteen years ago, and was somewhat more active than I am at present, I used frequently to scale the rock three or four times a day without the aid of a rope or a ladder; without any assistance in fact, whatsoever. During my late visits I have found it more convenient to ascend and descend by the help of ropes where the track lies up a precipitate cleft, and to throw a plank over those chasms where a false step in leaping across would be fatal. On reaching the recess which contains the Persian text ... ladders are indispensable ... and even with ladders there is considerable risk, for the foot-ledge is so narrow, about eighteen inches or at most two feet in breadth ... the upper inscription can only be copied by standing on the topmost step of the ladder with no other support than steadying the body against the rock with the left arm, while the left hand holds the note-book and the right arm is employed with the pencil.

'In this position', Rawlinson adds laconically, 'I copied all the upper inscriptions, and the interest of the occupation entirely did away with any sense of danger.'

He was thus able to copy the Old Persian inscription, but had greater difficulty with the Elamite inscription, which, incidentally, he called Scythic; but the real difficulties began when he tried to make a transcript of the Babylonian version. I quote Rawlinson's words again:

The writing can be copied by the aid of a good telescope from below, but I long despaired of obtaining a cast of the inscription; for I found it quite beyond my powers of climbing to reach the spot where it was engraved, and the cragsmen of the place, who were accustomed to track the mountain goats over the entire face of the mountain, declared the particular block inscribed with the Babylonian legend to be unapproach-able. At length however, a wild Kurdish boy, who had come from a distance volunteered to make the attempt ... the boy's first move was to squeeze himself up a cleft in the rock ... he drove a wooden peg firmly in to the cleft, fastened a rope to this. It then remained to him to cross over to the cleft by hang-ing on with his toes and fingers to the slight inequalities ... in this he succeeded, passing over a distance of twenty feet of almost smooth perpendicular rock in a manner which to a looker-on appeared quite miraculous. ... He had brought a rope with him attached to the first peg, and now, driving in a second, he was enabled to swing himself right over the project-ing mass of rock. Here, with a short ladder, he formed a swing-ing seat, like a painter's cradle, and, fixed upon this seat, he took down under my direction the paper cast of the Babylonian translation of the records of Darius which is now in the Royal Asiatic Society's Rooms, and which is almost of equal value for the interpretation of the Assyrian inscriptions as was the Greek translation on the Rosetta Stone for the intelligence of the hieroglyphic texts of Egypt.[45]

The wild Kurdish boy 'who had come from a distance' is one of my most favourite characters in the history of ar-chaeology. Rawlinson himself is another. He retired to the Residency in Baghdad with his copies and worked away at the decipherment and 'in order to enable himself to con-tinue working in the hot weather, built a little shelter at the bottom of the garden overlooking the river, and over this shelter water was continually being pumped.' He was a great character: Sir Wallis Budge tells a story that when he visited Baghdad in the nineties a Turkish official there, speaking of Rawlinson, said the following:

He lived here for twelve years, and each year his power be-came stronger. And towards the end of his time, had he taken one dog, and put his English hat on his head, and sent the dog to the *Serai*, all the people in the Bazaar would have made way for him and bowed to him. And the soldiers would have stood still and presented arms to him as he passed.[46]

The adventure with the Kurdish boy was in 1847. Ten years before, Rawlinson had succeeded in translating the first two paragraphs of the cuneiform inscription in Old Persian. In 1846 the Royal Asiatic Society published in two volumes his *The Persian Cuneiform Inscription at Behistun*, which was a complete translation of the Old Persian text, and in the same year, Dr Edward Hincks published an independent translation in the *Transactions of the Royal Irish Academy*.

When the Babylonian inscription was available, Rawlinson, Hincks and others including Oppert, de Saulcy and Fox Talbot, worked at its decipherment; soon this was done and the key to Babylonian and Assyrian obtained. But not everyone was satisfied that this was so. When, in 1857, Rawlinson translated for the British Museum an inscription on a cylinder of Tiglath Pileser I, there was some discussion and before publication it was decided to ask Hincks, Fox Talbot and Oppert to translate the inscription independently – and this they did. Rawlinson's translation and the three others were sent in sealed envelopes to the President of the Royal Asiatic Society, who had them examined by a select Committee. The Committee reported that the translations were so alike that there could be no longer any doubt that the true key to the decipherment of cuneiform writing had been found.

This was, in the first place, the key to the cuneiform writing of the Babylonians and Assyrians: it took Mesopotamian history back to 2000 B.C. But it was also a key to something else – to the Sumerians, whose existence in the land of Shinar no one at that time suspected. Except perhaps for Edward Hincks who, with great acumen, pointed out that the Semitic-speaking Babylonians could not have been the originators of the cuneiform form of writing which they themselves used. Babylonian, he argued, was a syllabic writing; and he thought that the cuneiform script was borrowed from an earlier people without syllabic writing. In this he was right, but he posed the question: Who were these people? Were they possibly earlier people who lived in the south of Mesopotamia?[47]

Serious excavation in Mesopotamia began in 1843 when P. E. Botta, the French consular agent at Mosul, started digging in the mound of Kuyunjik across the Tigris from Mosul. While excavating there late in 1842 and early in 1843 he learnt of sculptured stones found in the mound of Khorsabad, fourteen miles to the north, and at the end of March began work there; within a week he had discovered the remains of a huge Assyrian palace with large sculptured slabs and cuneiform inscriptions; at once he sent a telegram to Paris, '*Ninève est retrouvé.*'

Actually Botta was mistaken: Khorsabad was not Nineveh but Dur-Sharrukin, the city of one of the greatest Assyrian kings, Sargon II (721–705 B.C.), and it was Sargon the Second's palace that Botta had found: Nineveh was in fact the site of Kuyunjik which he had abandoned. But this did not matter; what mattered was that the spade was being used to examine the *tells* of Mesopotamia. In 1845 Layard began work at Nimrud, and in the 1850s Botta was succeeded by Place, and Layard by his former assistant Hormuzd Rassam.

Mesopotamian excavation had begun, though admittedly it was often very badly carried out, and no more than a scramble for antiques. Layard himself described his object in excavating at Nimrud as 'to obtain the largest possible number of well-preserved objects of art at the least possible outlay of time and money', and Rassam's work was in the words of Seton Lloyd 'an undignified scramble for archaeological loot'.[48]

Excavation in the south of Mesopotamia – homeland of the Sumerians – also began at this time. At the end of 1849 two Englishmen, W. K. Loftus and H. A. Churchill, rode across the deserts and marshes of southern Mesopotamia from the Euphrates to the Tigris and they saw the great Sumerian *tells* and, to their great surprise, the marks of former prosperity and intensive cultivation. Let me quote briefly from what Loftus wrote of Warka:

The desolation and solitude of Warka are even more striking than the scene presented by Babylon itself. There is no life for miles around. No river glides in grandeur at the base of its mounds, no green dates flourish near its ruins. . . . A blade of grass, or an insect, finds no existence there. The shrivelled lichen alone, clinging to the weathered surface of the broken brick, seems to glory in its universal dominion over these barren walls. Of all the desolate pictures I have ever beheld, that of Warka incomparably surpasses all.[49]

Loftus visited many of the *tells* in this region of southern Mesopotamia which, he said, 'from our childhood we have been led to regard as the cradle of the human race' – a curious sentence and presumably not a percipient guess at the Sumerians as the first to create a civilization, but a reference to the Garden of Eden. 'I know nothing more exciting or impressive,' he wrote, 'than the first sight of one of those great Chaldean piles looming in solitary grandeur from the surrounding plains and marshes. A thousand thoughts and surmises concerning its past eventful history and origin – its gradual rise and rapid fall – naturally present themselves to the mind of the spectator.' In 1850 Loftus began excavations at Warka, where he found a section of

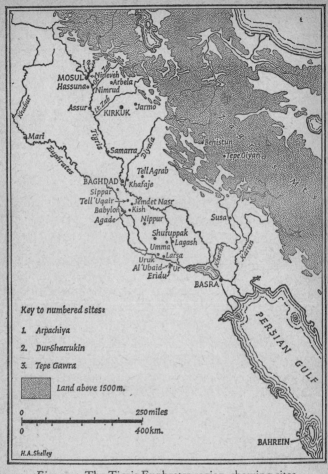

Key to numbered sites:

1. Arpachiya

2. Dur-Sharrukin

3. Tepe Gawra

Land above 1500m.

0   250 miles

0   400km.

H.A.Shelley

Figure 4. The Tigris-Euphrates region, showing sites

walling decorated with coloured mosaics of terracotta cones, and some cuneiform tablets. He then dug at other sites like Senkera, where he found terraces of kiln-baked brick and more clay tablets with cuneiform writing. He was not a scientific excavator – indeed who was at that time? Loftus frankly admitted that in excavating Warka he was actuated by 'a nervous desire to find important large museum pieces'; but however that may be, Rawlinson was able to work on the clay tablets. He identified Senkera as the ancient city of Larsa (the Biblical Ellarsar), and Warka as the Biblical Erech: 'And Cush begat Nimrud. And the beginning of his kingdom was Babel, and Erech, and Accad and Calneh, in the land of Shinar.' (*Genesis*, x, 10).

In 1854–5, J. E. Taylor, the British Vice-Consul at Basra, began excavating Tell Mukayyar and a group of mounds south of this at Tell-Abu-Shahrein. Rawlinson was able to identify the first site as Ur – Ur of the Chaldees, birthplace of Abraham – and the second as Eridu. The land of Shinar had been found and four of its ancient cities – Erech, Larsa, Ur and Eridu, also. We have said that Hincks, with great acumen, had argued for a pre-Babylonian people from whom the Babylonians borrowed their cuneiform writing. In 1869 Oppert boldly identified these non-Semitic pre-Babylonian people as the Sumerians. The finds of Loftus and Taylor were of these Sumerians, but Oppert's theory that the Sumerians had been in Iraq before the Babylonians and Assyrians was not widely accepted. Indeed there was nothing to show that the finds at Ur, Eridu, and elsewhere were much older, if older at all, than the palaces which Botta and Layard were digging near Mosul. The south Mesopotamian discoveries at first attracted little attention: they had yielded no great monumental sculpture. What was needed was some sensational discovery of aesthetic beauty before the world would interest itself or believe in the Sumerians.

That sensational discovery was made by Ernest de Sarzec, the French Consul in Basra. In 1874 some Arabs informed him that stone statuettes could be found in a place called Telloh, and in 1877 he dug trial trenches in this mound and found a number of fine diorite statues and many cuneiform inscriptions. He took them to Paris and sold them to the Louvre, and afterwards continued digging at the site intermittently, now under the auspices of the Louvre, until 1900. He was able to show that this was the Sumerian city of Lagash; his finds included many archaic sculptures of the late third millennium B.C., including the famous portrait statues of Gudea, the seventh Governor of Lagash – his date was some time in the period 2100 to 2000 B.C. The numerous statues and inscriptions of Gudea [Plates 7, 8] provided without any doubt the finest examples of Sumerian art and literature, and the discoveries of de Sarzec created sensations similar to those made by the discoveries of Botta at Khorsabad and Layard at Nineveh. The Louvre Catalogue of 1901 described Lagash as 'the Pompeii of early Babylonian antiquity', and de Genouillac said, 'C'est Telloh qui nous a révélé les Sumériens.' True, but they were not only revealed – they were found to be interesting and exciting. Not only were they old, and mentioned in the Bible – always a help in the nineteenth century when it seemed that those 'subterranean sciences' of geology and archaeology were undermining faith – but they were revealed as great artists practising a new art; that is to say, an art which was different from the familiar conventional ancient arts such as those of Greece and Rome and Egypt.

By 1900 the Sumerians had arrived, and by that year, too, their language was well understood. In this century we have seen the intensive and accurate revelation of the Sumerians by the spade and the skill of the translator of Sumerian. I single out two great moments in the twentieth-century excavation of this ancient people. In 1922 a joint expedition of the British Museum and the University Museum of Pennsylvania under the direction of Sir Leonard Woolley, as he later became, dug at Ur and in 1926 found the great cemetery with its Royal Tombs. The discovery of these tombs [Plates 10–13] with their splendid treasures of gold and lapis lazuli and their remarkable evidence of funerary ritual caused a sensation comparable with Schliemann's discoveries at Mycenae and the discovery of Tutankhamen's tomb. If the Sumerians were 'discovered' by 1900 there were still few people who had heard of them. By 1930 they had been added to the small collection of ancient peoples of whom nearly everyone had heard something. This was due in part to the sensational nature of the Ur excavations, but also to the clear and skilful popular writing of Woolley about his finds there.[50]

The second moment relates to the 1946–7 excavations at Eridu by the Iraq Government Directorate of Antiquities under the direction of Sayyid Fuad Safar. The site of Eridu-Tell-Abu-Shahrein had been, as we have said, dug by Taylor ninety years before. Taylor had been baffled by deep accumulations of sand, and hampered in the same way as were two British expeditions of this century by dust storms, by the general insecurity of the country and by great difficulties of communication. The excavations in the forties of this century however triumphed over these difficulties and revealed in Eridu the earliest Sumerian city, and perhaps the earliest city in the world. We have quoted the sentence in *Genesis*, x, which mentioned Erech – that is, Warka – as one of the old cities in the land of Shinar. The Babylonian

Legend of Creation is more specific: it says, 'All the lands were sea; then Eridu was made.' And in Sumerian literature the god Enki dwelt at Eridu, and Enki was the god of the Abyss who dwelt in his shrine on the shores of the deep, which was divided as a preliminary to creation.

It has been my intention to introduce you deliberately to the Sumerians by going back to the time when we knew nothing of what their *tells* and cuneiform writing meant, so that you can appreciate how our knowledge of man's first civilization was achieved. In the next chapter I shall outline the detail of the archaeological finds and it will be seen that by level IV at Uruk we can say that civilization had been born – the first civilization in the history of man.

The lowest building levels at Eridu – that is to say, Eridu XVIII to XV (the numbering is from the top down) – revealed small houses and shrines built of mud-brick to rectangular plans. This phase, the earliest in the known occupation of southern Mesopotamia, dates back to about five thousand years B.C. The people were settled agriculturists and peasants, and at this stage the civilization of the Sumerians is far ahead. The second and next phase in the prehistory of southern Mesopotamia is called after the site of Hajji Muhammad; it began, perhaps, around 4750 B.C., and at Eridu it occupies five building levels. This phase had sites all over southern Mesopotamia and was even better represented in Susiana and Luristan. It develops into the next, the third phase, named after the site of Al 'Ubaid. A C14 date from Warka suggests that the early 'Ubaid phase was fully fledged by 4350 B.C. The people of the 'Ubaid phase developed and spread over the whole of Mesopotamia.

Now, the existence of people in southern Mesopotamia in this phase without efficient irrigation is quite unthinkable. The rich and fertile plain was being tilled and it became overpopulated, so that the 'Ubaid people from the south moved up the Tigris and Euphrates in search of new land.

Twenty-five years ago the picture of the 'Ubaid people was rather that of primitive marsh-dwellers living in reed huts, hunting, fishing and practising sporadic agriculture like the Ma'dan or Marsh Arabs of today. Now all that picture is changed, and the Eridu excavations of 1946-7 were largely responsible for that change. The people of Al 'Ubaid were using copper and casting axes; gold made its appearance at the end of the period, their agriculture was efficient and they engaged in extensive trade. If we do not give them the name of civilization at least they were a proto-civilization, a civilization in the making, because they already had towns; and this is obvious from two things: first, their large cemeteries (that at Eridu contained over a thousand graves), and secondly, the monumental temples that now appeared for the first time – the ceremonial centres which we have said by definition are one of the prerequisites of civilized society. Built of mud-brick and sometimes on stone foundations they dominated the cities from the top of the mounds. At Eridu, set on mud-brick platforms made by filling in earlier buildings, a flight of steps gave access to a door in the long side of the building. The outside was ornamented with elaborate projections and recesses, a characteristic of all later Sumerian sacred buildings. At Eridu we find the beginning of that most characteristic feature of early Mesopotamian archaeology – the temple tower or ziggurat. We are already within sight – perhaps talking distance is the right word – of the Tower of Babel. And we are in a town or small city – Professor Max Mallowan thinks that even before 4000 B.C. Eridu was a place of several thousand souls.[51]

In the established archaeological sequence of southern Mesopotamia the 'Ubaid phase is succeeded by the Uruk phase which lasted from 3800 or 3700 to 3200 B.C.: the culture of Uruk is already in its maturity by about 3500 B.C. The site of Uruk itself consists of eighteen levels observed by excavations in a deep sounding in the precincts of the ceremonial centre – the ziggurat of E-anna. This deep pit, or *sondage*, was about twenty metres in depth and contained in it the accumulated debris of settlements beginning with the people of 'Ubaid times. I had already said that archaeologists sometimes label their levels from top to bottom, but at other times from the bottom, the earliest level, up. Uruk is another example of the bottom-to-top method: the first and oldest level at that site is XVIII, and the full development of the site is in level Uruk IV. At this time Sumerian pottery and architecture were at a high state of development, and contemporary with the great temples of Uruk IV we find the earliest abundant evidence of writing. A civilization has been born: the first civilization in the history of man – the Sumerian civilization, and its date was perhaps 3200 B.C., five thousand years ago.

CHAPTER THREE

THE SUMERIANS AND THE
ORIGIN OF CIVILIZATION

IT was, then, some five thousand years ago that civilization began in southern Mesopotamia. In the last chapter we said that by the fourth Uruk phase (Uruk IV), somewhere between 3200 and 3100 B.C., we were without any doubt dealing with a society that was civilized according to the definitions of civilization which we are adopting in this book. There were cities, specialized craftsmen, co-operative irrigation works, ceremonial centres, writing – and many more things which make the proto-literate society of Uruk and Jemdet Nasr civilized in the meaningful historical and archaeological use of that word. And that civilization, which in terms of archaeological levels and periods is Uruk IV and Jemdet Nasr, is Sumerian.[52]

The Early Dynastic period of Sumer covers the part of the third millennium from 2800 to 2400 B.C. and ends with the conquest of Sumer by a Semitic king of the North, Sargon I of Akkad. Then there was a Sumerian 'Renaissance' from 2120 B.C. until Ur was destroyed at the end of the third millennium B.C. This was certainly not the end of Sumerian civilization but it was the end of Sumer as an independent ruling nation. So, when we talk of the first civilization of man, the Sumerian civilization, we mean that civilized society, that highly developed and sophisticated culture which flourished in southern Mesopotamia from the second half of the fourth millennium B.C. to the end of the third millennium.

Let us go over the basic characteristics of this first civilized society. First, the Sumerians were city-dwellers. Their cities were surrounded by brick walls and a ditch and dominated by temples and ziggurats set on high platforms. Outside the walls were gardens, fields, dykes, canals and harbours. The walls of Erech encompassed two square miles, and Lagash is reported as having thirty-six thousand males, probably adult males, so that it might well have been a town or city of eighty to a hundred thousand people – approximately the size of the modern English towns of Oxford or Cambridge or Norwich. It has been estimated that at the height of its expansion half a million people lived within the four square miles of Ur, and that Kish, Eridu, Lagash and Nippur at their greatest moments might have had comparable populations.

Each city was the centre of a little city-state : Sumer was organized on the basis of fifteen to twenty small city-states each politically autonomous, but all economically interdependent. Each city-state in turn tried to get control of others, or of the whole federation : inter-city-state wars occurred but they were not major affairs and were usually about administrative matters like the ownership of land or irrigation rights.

The Sumerian cities or large towns were based on a flourishing agriculture ; barley was the main crop, but wheat, emmer, millet and sesame were also grown, and, of course, the date-palm, 'its feet in the water and its head in the scorching sun'. There were fruits and vegetables, and domesticated cattle and sheep. It should be borne in mind that at the present day the plain watered by the Tigris and Euphrates is a rich farming land and that it was much richer before extensive salination took place. The whole population of the area could easily live on the produce of the land

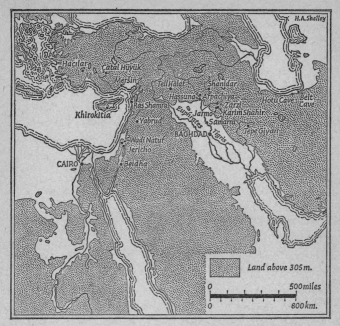

Figure 5. The Near East, showing principal sites

and barter the surplus for what they wanted from abroad. It is important to remember too that this was no subsistence agriculture; it was a well-organized agriculture with a complex system of irrigation canals. Irrigation and drainage involved complicated and co-operative efforts requiring control, organization, and a centralized society.

In Sumerian, and for that matter Akkadian, there seems to be no distinction between the words that we in English apply to different sizes of settlements – city, town, village, hamlet. *Uru* and *alu* are all these things although the villages grouped around a city were called *uru barra*. In the settlement there were specialized craftsmen in their work-shops, as well as granaries and magazines. There were smiths, glaziers, jewellers and seal-cutters. The so-called Royal Graves of Ur give us a picture of Sumerian art and craftsmanship between 3000 and 2800 B.C., and show that at that time the Sumerians were masters of metallurgy, stone-carving, glass-working, filigree work and carpentry.

One of their main crafts was metallurgy. Native copper worked cold is attested at Çatal Hüyük in Anatolia in the seventh millennium B.C.[53] In the 'Ubaid period of Mesopotamia, that is to say certainly from 4400 to 4300 B.C., metal was common and cast axes of copper were being made at least in the north of the country, and objects of gold make their first appearance. From at least the beginnings of Dynastic times the Sumerian smith knew how to alloy copper and tin to produce bronze, and the first discovery of this alloy – so important in the late prehistoric and proto-historic world – may well have been due to Sumerian smiths. They certainly understood the closed mould and the *cire-perdue* method of casting, which they probably invented. The earliest certain example of *cire-perdue* casting is the elaborate model of a car or chariot drawn by four onagers from Tell Agrab: this dates from Early Dynastic II, that is to say, about the middle of the third millennium B.C. It also seems likely that it was the metallurgical expertise of the Sumerians that included the invention of the socket. They had been using gold since 'Ubaid times: they also used silver and lead, and from 3000 B.C. onwards occasional objects of iron appear. The Sumerian smiths were clearly experimenting in metallurgy.[54]

There was no native metal in Mesopotamia: metal-working and many another craft involved extensive trade relations. The Sumerians got tin from eastern Iran, from

Asia Minor and Syria, and perhaps, although we cannot be certain about this, from Europe. They got gold from Elam, Cappadocia and the region of Antioch, while silver and lead came from the Taurus mountains and from Elam. Copper they obtained from Oman in the south of the Persian Gulf, and perhaps from the Caucasus as well. Oman was also the source of stone for querns and door-sockets and statues. Lapis lazuli came from Persia and Afghanistan, mother of pearl from the Persian Gulf, sank (or chank) shells from India, cedar and pine from the Lebanon Mountains of Syria and the Zagros Mountains of Iran. Thus the trade relations of the Sumerians were very wide from Asia Minor to India, and we know something about how this trade was carried out. By 2500 B.C. a colony, or a factory if you prefer the word, of Sumerians existed at Kanesh in Asia Minor, and this commercial and colonial outpost of the people of south Mesopotamia was arranging for the export of copper and silver and lead from mines in Anatolia. And, as we shall see in the next chapter, there were certainly commercial relations with the Indus cities to the east and with Egypt to the west.

Next in our list of the Sumerian contributions to the civilized world is the wheel. The Sumerians invented the wheel. First it was a potter's wheel: they made fine pottery on the wheel and baked it in complicated ovens and they knew the art of glazing, and incidentally we should mention here that the first glass also was Sumerian. Before 3000 B.C. they had used the wheel as a rotary device to make vehicles more mobile: they had heavy four-wheeled working waggons and lighter two-wheel carts which might have been used as battle cars or chariots; all these were solid-wheeled vehicles.[55]

The Sumerian towns had ceremonial centres of distinction

and importance. At the end of the Uruk phase at Erech, the *tell* – the accumulation of the settlements that had gone before – was as much as 60 feet high, and there was a gigantic temple dedicated to the goddess E-anna. This temple measured 245 feet by 100 and behind it was the ziggurat 35 feet high with a flight of steps leading to the summit, where there was a platform covered with asphalt on which was a smaller temple 73 feet long by 57 feet 6 inches. As Gordon Childe put it vividly. 'One is no longer standing in a village green but in the square of a cathedral city.'

These ceremonial centres and other places were served by a fine architecture. In dynastic times the Sumerians used plano-convex or pincushion-shaped bricks. It was the Sumerian architects who invented the brick column; theirs were the oldest columns in the world, inspired directly by the trunk of the date palm.

The centres of the Sumerian city-states were these ceremonial areas, the *temenos*, the citadel with the temples of the gods. Each city seems to have had a patron god, and among the Sumerian pantheon was a group of goddesses, all perhaps representing different aspects of the earth-mother goddess, one of the first and earliest of goddesses in human history. It was on the ziggurat, the staged tower or artificial mountain, that each year the Sumerians celebrated their most sacred ritual: at the new year a young priest and a young priestess were led to the ziggurat where in the presence of an officiating priest they consummated the symbolical union which according to Sumerian religion assured the success of the new season's crops. This done, they were killed and buried.

Contemporary with the great temples of Uruk IV we find the earliest evidence of writing. This writing was on clay tablets. There are 500 to 600 clay tablets or fragments of such tablets from Uruk IV, III and II, and this is the largest and earliest stratified collection of writing known to us. At first the signs were of objects, animate and inanimate, which were, we assume, important in the lives of the Sumerians – sheep, cows, cereals, temples, milk-pails, agricultural implements. They are mainly pictograms but there are exceptions, and in some instances the significance of the signs is still unknown. The writing of the Sumerians, their cuneiform or wedge-shaped writing, was done with a reed. The development of a syllabic script was the achievement of the Babylonians, and we mentioned in the last chapter that a shrewd scholar like Oppert was certain that Babylonian writing could not have been devised by a Semitic-speaking people but had been borrowed from earlier non-Semitic speakers – the Sumerians.

The earliest written documents of the Sumerians are not literature: they are not sagas, or legends of creation. They are domestic or commercial documents such as lists of deliveries of bread and beer to various people, ration lists, and lists of items delivered to temple and other officials. The first written documents of about 3500 B.C. are memos and receipts for cattle, milk, corn, sheep.

The Sumerians made many more inventions than we have space to enumerate, but there is one aspect of their inventive genius that must be mentioned briefly, namely their mathematics. They had a system of calendars and a well-thought-out system of mathematics, and had made many and accurate astronomical observations. The debt of Western civilization to the Sumerians is large, and in our list we should not omit positional numeration and the sexagesimal system by which we still divide our clocks and the circle. And, curiously enough, there are even a few

Sumerian words that we still use in English – cane, alcohol, dragoman, gypsum, myrrh, saffron and naphtha.

All these things and much besides certainly add up to a civilization, and, what is more, to the first civilization. So many things started among the cities of southern Mesopotamia that it is no surprise to find Kramer saying that Sumer had almost too many firsts. Certainly the vital contribution made by the Sumerians to the development of civilized life must be considered one of the greatest early achievements of man. We have some idea of what the Sumerians looked like and of their ordinary life. They were short in stature and had large curved noses. In their statues they represent themselves as bullet-headed people with big dark heads, long beards, but no moustaches. They dressed themselves in sheep-skins or garments of woven wool, and wore skirts with flounces. At their banquets they sat in groups and drank a sort of beer: a jar of this beer stood on the floor between them and they drank it through long metal tubes. They made music on harps of various kinds and shapes. For their amusements they wrestled and boxed, they hunted, and they raced in light two-wheeled carts or chariots to which four onagers, or wild asses, were yoked.

Who were the Sumerians and where did they come from? There has been, not unnaturally, a very great deal of discussion of this problem, and it is of course not merely the problem of where did the Sumerians come from, but the problem of whence came the people who created man's first civilization. I quoted at the beginning of the last chapter the words from *Genesis*, xi: 'And it came to pass, as they journeyed from the east, that they found a plain in the land of Shinar; and they dwelt there.' Berosus, writing in the fourth/third century B.C., described a race of monsters, half-men and half-fish which, led by one Oannes, came out of the Persian Gulf, and, settling in the coast towns of Sumer, introduced the arts of writing, of agriculture and or working in metal. 'All the things that make for the amelioration of life were bequeathed to men by Oannes, and since that time no further inventions have been made.'

We should at once remember three things in discussing this problem of Sumerian origins: first, that the earliest building style of the Sumerians was based on a tradition of working in timber; secondly, that the Sumerian gods are always represented as standing on mountains – the ziggurat is an artificial mountain. But in the third place we must bear in mind that archaeology can now tell us that the earliest settlements in southern Mesopotamia do not, probably, go further back than 5000 B.C. at the most and that the first agriculturists and the first village life was earlier than this in areas outside the land of the twin rivers, for example in the north of Mesopotamia, in Iran, in Jordan and in Turkey.

It was groups of these earlier and earliest agriculturists who settled in the flood plain of the Tigris-Euphrates, and, to use Robert Braidwood's evocative phrase, 'fingered their way' down the rivers to the Persian Gulf. I think that no one would now challenge this very general statement, namely that the 'Ubaid people came into southern Mesopotamia from outside, although they would disagree about which area these people came from, and they might want to argue for fresh outside influences between the first villages and Uruk IV. Naturally, it is not possible to be dogmatic in this matter and say that the people who were in southern Mesopotamia before 3500 B.C. were definitely Sumerians. We cannot label people with a historical name before that name occurs in writing. But let me put this another way: the Sumerians are the people who lived in southern Mesopotamia probably from 5000 B.C. onwards. When the light of history shines on them, that is to say the light of written history provided by the records in cuneiform writing which they had themselves invented, they were calling themselves Sumerians.

Let us go back again to *Genesis*, and this time to the Creation story as told in *Genesis*, i:

In the beginning God created the heaven and the earth. And the earth was without form, and void; and darkness was upon the face of the deep. And the Spirit of God moved upon the face of the waters. And God said, Let there be light: and there was light ... And God said, Let there be a firmament in the midst of the waters, and let it divide the waters from the waters. And God made the firmament, and divided the waters which were under the firmament from the waters which were above the firmament: and it was so ... And God said, Let the waters under the heaven be gathered together unto one place, and let the dry land appear: and it was so. And God called the dry land Earth; and the gathering together of the waters called he Seas ... And God said, Let the earth bring forth grass, the herb yielding seed, and the fruit tree yielding fruit after his kind ...

We are here concerned with the affairs of this third day – admittedly a notional day, a stage in the evolution of man and the world, if you like to put it that way. For many centuries, of course, theologians and others thought that this was a correct account of prehistoric origins, in that it had been inspired by a supernatural being and had supernatural authority. I do not think that at the present day any but the most rabid fundamentalists still hold this view. From 1876 onwards Babylonian accounts of the Creation have been published which reveal the origin of the *Genesis* account. The longest of these is known as *Enuma Elish* from its two first words which mean 'when on high', and was written in the early part of the second millennium B.C. It survives almost complete on seven cuneiform tablets. There is another account written both in Babylonian and Sumerian on a tablet discovered at Sippar dating from the sixth century B.C. I quote a few sentences from it:

All lands were sea
Then there was a movement on the midst of the sea;
At that time Eridu was made ...
Marduk laid a reed on the face of the waters,
He formed dust and poured it out beside the reed
That he might cause the gods to dwell in the dwelling of their
   hearts' desire
He formed mankind
With him the goddess Aruru created the seed of mankind.
The beasts of the field and living things in the field he formed
The Tigris and Euphrates he created and established them in
   their place:
Their name he proclaimed in goodly manner
The grass, the rush of the marsh, the reed and the forest he
   created,
The lands, the marshes and the swamps;
The wild cow and her young, the lamb of the fold,
Orchards and forests;
The he-goat and the mountain-goat ...
The Lord Marduk built a dam beside the sea ...
Reeds he formed, trees he created;
Bricks he laid, buildings he erected;
Houses he made, cities he built ...
Erech he made ...

There is only one comment I wish to add here to this fascinating Mesopotamian epic of creation which is the source of the *Genesis* creation legend, and that is a remark of Gordon Childe's. It was no divine being, he said, who brought dry land out of the waters, established the Tigris and

Euphrates in their places, created fields and orchards and forests: it was the hard-working proto-Sumerians.

We must, then, substitute the proto-Sumerians for Yahweh or Marduk; and we know what they did and when they did it, namely in southern Mesopotamia they created for the first time in human history a civilization where before there had only been villages. They created an urban literate society; they created the first civilization. We know the answers to the questions what and when and where; but we also want to know how and why civilization was created in Mesopotamia.

You will not be surprised to be told that a great number of theories have been put forward to explain the how and the why of Sumerian civilization. The first group of theories may be called the geographical explanations, and among these we may list the so-called propinquity theory of Brooks. This theory argued that everything was so lovely in the garden – to put it crudely, and, incidentally, I think Brooks unconsciously meant the Garden of Eden – that it was all bound to happen. Here in Mesopotamia were wild wheat and barley, wild sheep and goats and a fertile river delta; given all these things together, and civilization was inevitable. But Brooks was conflating thousands of years of human history: he was conflating the origins of agriculture in the Near East as a whole with the origins of civilization in Sumer. The same conflation has been made by those such as Arnold Toynbee, who like to think of a similar simple explanation accounting for the origins of Egyptian and Mesopotamian civilization, viewed in terms of the end of the Ice Age.

The simplest account of the geographical origins of civilization in the ancient Near East has often been set out: as the ice sheets retreated across Europe and the rain belt that was over the Sahara moved north, the hunters and food-gatherers who had been happy to live in the Saharan grasslands were forced to migrate, south into Africa, north following the retreating ice to Europe; or to settle in the river valleys of the Nile and the Tigris-Euphrates, turn into agriculturists, and so, encouraged by the fertility of these river valleys, to prosper and lay the basis of civilization. Put in this bald fashion the story sounds improbable and grossly over-simplified; and in any case, it was not, as we now know, in the river valleys of Egypt and Mesopotamia that incipient agriculture and the beginnings of village life took place.

But, even so, we shall have to agree that the river valleys and the floods had something to do with the development of higher barbarian culture into what we term civilization. It cannot be an accident that the four ancient civilizations of the Old World are based on the Tigris-Euphrates, the Nile, the Indus and the Yellow River. To say this is not to hint at any form of geographical determinism, but to say that the geographical environment of these river valleys and alluvial plains was an important factor in the genesis of the civilizations: it provided possibilities. Echoing Herodotus's famous sentence that 'Egypt is the gift of the Nile', Georges Roux declares that 'in many respects it can also be said of Mesopotamia that it is a gift of the twin river'.[56]

The scholar who has written most in English about the particular problem of the origins of civilization and archaeology is Vere Gordon Childe, and he was certainly one of the most formative and important figures in the historical development of thought about archaeological facts and the light they throw on the beginnings of civilized societies. In 1936 Childe wrote a small book entitled *Man Makes Himself*, and he followed this up six years later with *What*

Happened in History, a title which was deliberately provoking to the ordinary historian with a restricted perspective of the past because it ends with Byzantium – indeed the last chapter is called 'The Decline and Fall of the Ancient World'.

Childe argued that there had been three great revolutions in human history; the first two of these he called the Neolithic and Urban Revolutions, while the third was the Industrial Revolution. In many ways what he was propounding in the thirties and early forties of this century is still true, but we would now want to modify it in several ways, largely owing to the increase of our archaeological knowledge since his death; and it is a quarter of a century since Childe wrote *What Happened in History*. The first modification is that these processes were not revolutionary: revolution suggests something that happened quickly and purposefully. The changes from food-gathering to food-producing and from self-sufficient village life to literate towns were evolutionary rather than revolutionary changes: they took long periods of time and they were not so much purposeful as the practical application of discoveries and inventions that were often made accidentally. To say this, of course, is in no way to belittle the importance of these changes. Secondly, I do not like the use of the words Neolithic and Urban to describe these great changes. The term Neolithic was invented by Sir John Lubbock for what was conceived, a hundred years ago, as the second half of the Stone Age, and it was still being defined in the archaeological textbooks of the first quarter of this century as a stage of human culture distinguished by polished stone axes, pottery, domesticated animals and the cultivation of grain – this was the quadrivium of the Neolithic.[57] We now know so much more about the period 10,000 to 4000 B.C. in the Near East and from

5000 to 1000 B.C. in America, and we have found societies evolving from food-gathering and hunter-fisher groups into societies with only one, or two, or three, of these four diagnostic features. The result of this, incidentally, has been the creation of strange and unnecessary phrases like 'Pre-Pottery Neolithic' and 'Aceramic Neolithic'. The truth is that the word Neolithic can no longer be defined in a sensible or meaningful way.

The trouble with the word Urban, and with referring as Childe did to the Urban Revolution, is that this word is to most people overlaid with ideas of conurbations, skyscrapers, factories, underground railways and double-decker buses, with commuters and big business. I would prefer to use the English version of the Greek word *synoecismus* which was used by Thucydides and meant the union of several towns and villages under one capital city. Garner in 1902 spoke of the time 'when the town was first formed by the synoecism of the neighbouring villages.'[58]

My third objection to Childe's general thesis lies in the model of prehistory which was informing his thought and writing. It was a model which, while eschewing the extravagant hyper-diffusionism of the Egyptocentrics like Elliot Smith and Perry, and Sumerocentrics like Raglan, nevertheless had at the back of it the idea that there was only one Neolithic Revolution and only one Urban Revolution and that both of them took place in the most ancient Near East. These matters we will return to for further discussion in the last chapter.

In addition to his general thesis, Childe gave his specific reasons why the urban civilization of Sumer came into existence, and these we can consider quite apart from any general idea of the number of times that urbanization or the *synoecismus*-process took place in human history. Childe did not propound a geographical determinism, but a materialist determinism. He was quite sure that the origin of Sumerian civilization was due to a series of technological discoveries. He wrote: 'Metallurgy, the wheel, the ox-cart, the pack-ass, and the sailing ship provided the foundations for a new organization. Without it the new materials would remain luxuries, the new crafts would not function, the new devices would be just conveniences.' And yet he was uncertain about allowing the whole process of the birth of the first civilization to be explained by a catalogue of technological inventions and discoveries, and conceded that 'the alluvial valleys of the great rivers offered a more exacting environment'.

It seems to me that the alluvial plain of the Tigris and Euphrates offered an exciting as well as an exacting environment. The groups of people who fingered their way down from the higher lands where incipient agriculture had developed and the first villages came into existence found themselves in a very rich micro-environment and one that was liable to floods and which needed irrigation by canals, and cooperative enterprises. Out of this fertility and this cooperation the villages prospered and grew, and the miracle of the first civilization happened: the Sumerian synoecism took place. But it was not the environment that caused this first civilization in human history to happen; it was the Sumerians themselves. In 1932 Lucien Febvre published his *Geographical Introduction to History*, and in that very important book he criticizes with wit and good humour the excesses of the geographical determinists. What the physical environment provides, he argued, was possibilities, and it is in terms of this possibilism that we should envisage the emergence of the Sumerian civilization. The Sumerians, or, if you like, the proto-Sumerians, settled in the environment provided by the Tigris-Euphrates deltaic plain and took advantage of the possibilities of that environment to grow and prosper. But we must not delude ourselves into thinking that all one has to do is produce possibilities and they will automatically be accepted and used. As our discussion proceeds we shall see that there were many areas of possibilities existing in the world that did not in fact produce civilizations.

The genius of the people must be seen against the background of the possibilities of their geographical environment. It was, as Childe said, not God but the hard-working Sumerians who created the land between the two rivers. It was the genius of the Sumerians that invented the wheel, glass, bronze, writing, the calendar and the city. It may have been something special in their make-up, and I cannot do better than end this chapter with a sentence from Kramer: 'The psychological factor responsible to no little extent for both the material and cultural achievements of the Sumerians was an all-pervading and deeply ingrained drive for pre-eminence and prestige, for victory and success.'

CHAPTER FOUR

EGYPT AND THE INDUS
VALLEY

THE subject of the preceding two chapters was the Sumerians, the first civilized people in the story of the development of human society. We now turn to the Egyptians and to the people who created the Indus civilization. It may seem strange to group together into one chapter these two early and important civilizations, but it is not the purpose of this book to describe and analyse the development of man's early civilizations. Our theme is simply the light which archaeology throws on the phenomena of the origins of man's first civilizations. It is very easy to read in a wide variety of books descriptions of the nature of the ancient Egyptian and ancient Indus civilizations;[59] our concern is how, why and when these two civilizations happened. Were they independent manifestations of the human spirit as was Sumer? Were they the product of the genius of the people living in the valleys of the Nile and the Indus? Or did they derive something – inspiration, leaders, people – from Sumer? In examining this problem we shall spend more time over India than over Egypt because Egypt is, of all the seven early civilizations we are discussing in this book, the best known to the ordinary reader. He will at least have seen photographs of the Pyramids and the Sphinx, and have heard of Tutankhamen and Akhenaten.

The real difficulty is that so many think they know something about the ancient Egyptians, as they think they do about the ancient Britons, though in fact they know peril-

ously little. But most people have heard Egypt described –
even if they do not know that it was Herodotus who coined
the phrase – as the gift of the Nile and this may be the real
clue to the origin of Egyptian civilization. For that matter
the existence of rivers may be the real clue to the origins of
the four ancient Old World civilizations: civilizations
which may have arisen from the skilful utilization by gifted
people of the possibilities of success and failure offered by
the fertile river valleys of the Nile, the Tigris-Euphrates,
the Indus and the Yellow River. But let us return to our
immediate topic, Egypt. The Nile Valley consists of a sea-
sonally inundated flood plain, with low-lying sand and
gravel wastes bordering the flood plain, and then moun-
tainous escarpments along the margins.[60] The Nile flood
rises in July with the falling of the tropical rains on the
Abyssinian highlands, and subsides in November, after
which time the seeds can germinate and the crops ripen in
the warmth of the Egyptian winter and spring.

In Mesopotamia, as we have seen, the first centres of civilization were in the south of the country, at Ur, Eridu and
Erech; they then moved northwards. We are told that this
is because of salination, the salting-up of the southern flood
plain. Mesopotamian civilization began in the south and
moved north leaving an empty area behind it. This was not
so in Egypt. Egypt is described geographically as falling into
two parts: Lower Egypt, comprising the Delta, and Upper
Egypt, the South. What happened to Egyptian civilization
was that it grew and grew, but it did not move: there never
was an area of Egypt deserted because of salination. Most of
Upper Egypt was an area where people could and did live
from the second half of the fourth millennium B.C., and
from Dynasty III, if not earlier, it was divided into *nomes*
or administrative provinces. Lower Egypt, the Delta, was

conquered and occupied gradually – perhaps the complete conquest did not occur until Ptolemaic times – but there never was a shift in focus. Egypt just grew.

Both the Sumerians and the Egyptians created civilizations based on irrigation, but it would be a mistake to conceptualize irrigation, and believe it to be one thing in all places. Indeed it is a very different thing in Mesopotamia and in Egypt. In the land of the twin rivers it was a process of making canals; there were canal banks above the fields, the water drained away on to the fields, and sank into the soil, and this is why, in due course, the south Mesopotamian fields had to be abandoned because of salination. This never happened in Egypt: Egypt was the gift of the Nile in the sense that the Nile did do all the work – it all happened with the flooding of the Nile. In Egypt the mud dries out but the salt remains deep in the cracks and drains from the fields to the river.

When Napoleon invaded Egypt he took with him a special scientific staff, and among the many things which this staff was charged to do was to record the country's antiquities. Napoleon himself was interested in the visible antiquities of the remote Egyptian past, but we do not know whether, on the eve of the great battle of the Nile, he actually addressed his troops in the shadow of the Great Pyramid, and said, 'Soldiers, forty centuries of history look down on you.' He may have done this, or he may not: I like to believe that he did, and that this is the first example of the use of archaeology for political purposes.[61]

Napoleon's Egyptian scientific staff – 'the donkeys' as they were called by the military staff – included Dolomieu, the mineralogist whose name survives in the Dolomites, and Denon, the artist. They arrived in 1798 and, despite Nelson's destruction of the French fleet in Abukir Bay, the

French Institute was founded in Cairo. The staff of this Institute carried on its work with great energy and thoroughness: they did not excavate, but they described and drew, and they collected portable antiquities. When the French were compelled to evacuate Egypt in 1801 their collection of Egyptian works of art had to be surrendered to England, and therefore found its way to the British Museum and not to the Louvre as was originally intended. The French Institute in Cairo remained in the hands of the French and in due course produced the remarkable *Description de l'Égypte* (1799–1813). The most exciting object that came to the British Museum instead of the Louvre was the famous Rosetta Stone [Plate 23], found by accident in digging the foundations of a fort near Alexandria. It is a black basalt stone bearing inscriptions in Greek, demotic and hieroglyphics. The decipherment of the demotic and hieroglyphic inscriptions on the Rosetta Stone and on other monuments was carried out in the first decade of the nineteenth century: many people were involved in this but the two most important names were the Englishman Thomas Young, whose results were published in an article on Egypt in the 1818 edition of the *Encyclopaedia Britannica,* and Jean François Champollion, whose work was published in 1822.[62]

This decipherment was the key to ancient Egypt, at least as regards its literate past. But literacy, by definition and by fact, accompanies civilization. The origins of Egyptian civilization are buried in its pre-literate pre-dynastic past. In the reign of Ptolemy Philadelphus, an Egyptian high priest named Manetho wrote in Greek a history of Egypt, which now survives only in garbled summaries, and in extracts in the works of later authors. There are also epigraphic and archaeological lists of Pharaohs such as that on the Palermo

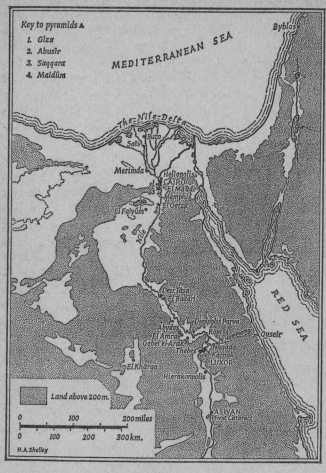

Figure 6. The Nile Valley, showing sites

Stone. From these and other sources detailed king-lists have been prepared, and it appears that about 3200 B.C. Upper and Lower Egypt were united under one king and that this was the beginning of the historic period in Egypt with main sites at Memphis, Saqqara, Giza and Abydos [Plates 15, 16]. The beginnings of the historic ancient civilization of Egypt are now conveniently and conventionally divided into the archaic period from 3200 and 2700 B.C. (including Dynasties I and II) and the Old Kingdom from 2700 to 2160 B.C. (comprising Dynasties III to VIII).

The first king of Egypt was Narmer, and he perhaps was also the semi-legendary Menes, the first Pharaoh, the man whose name the temple-guides told to Herodotus as the first king of Egypt. The palette of Narmer [Plate 20] shows him wearing the *desbret*, the red crown of Lower Egypt, on one side, and the *hedjet*, the white crown of Upper Egypt, on the other. A rebus seems to say: 'Pharaoh, the incarnation of the hawk-god Horus, with his strong right arm leads captive the Marsh-dwellers', and this is usually represented as commemorating the victory of a southern king over the north. In actual fact Narmer-Menes may have had a predecessor, King Scorpion, whose mace-head from Hierakonpolis dates from about 3225 B.C.[63]

Figure 7. The white and red crowns of the Pharaohs, representing Upper and Lower Egypt.

But, we ask, what went on in Egypt before the unification of south and north at the beginning of written history? Years of description and excavation followed upon the Napoleonic period of Egyptian archaeology: some of it was plain and unadorned tomb robbing and looting, but some was very good work. The Egypt Exploration Fund (later the Egypt Exploration Society) was founded in London in 1883, and its work in the field was directed by, as he later became, Sir Flinders Petrie. In 1883 Petrie wrote to Miss Amelia Edwards, the Secretary of the Fund: 'The prospect of excavating in Egypt is a most fascinating one to me, and I hope the results may justify my undertaking such a work.' They most certainly did. Petrie worked first on dynastic sites, and then, from 1894 onwards, on earlier sites of which Naqada is the most famous. Here he unearthed a cemetery of two thousand graves. The British Museum declined Petrie's offer of the type series from this cemetery on the ground that they were advised it was 'unhistoric rather than prehistoric'. In this they were wrongly advised, but the collection went to the Ashmolean Museum at Oxford, instead. In 1901 in his memoir on another site, Diospolis Parva, Petrie arranged the pre-dynastic (or prehistoric) material from Egypt systematically for the first time.[64]

There is no need here to go in detail into the classifications of Petrie and their subsequent alterations. Let us summarize what seems to have happened in the most general terms. Until the last ten years the general thesis in textbooks and lectures was that the Neolithic Revolution, that is to say the origins of agriculture and the domestication of animals, began in Egypt and in southern Mesopotamia, and that these Neolithic communities developed into literate cities. The only dispute was over which country the Neolithic Revolution and the Urban Revolution happened in first. Now archaeological research tells us that the earliest evidence for agriculture and the domestication of animals in the Old World occurs not in Egypt or southern Mesopotamia but in Palestine, southern Turkey, northern Mesopotamia and western Iran. There is now no longer any possibility of arguing the primacy of Egypt in this matter. The first agricultural communities in Egypt were later in date, and neither of the two wheats, nor barley, nor sheep or goats are native to Egypt in their wild state. The first peasant village agriculturists in Egypt and the Sudan occur as early perhaps as the fifth millennium B.C., and the higher arts and crafts were probably diffused to Egypt from south-west Africa. But the early societies of Egypt soon took on an African feel, and no one looking at the material remains of the early Egyptian communities that existed between say 5000 and 3000 B.C. can mistake them for western Asiatic societies.[65]

The question we are asking ourselves here is this: What happened to transform these Egyptian villages into the literate urban civilization of dynastic Egypt? Was it just a growth in prosperity, and a repetition of what we have seen happening in the delta of the Tigris-Euphrates? Was it an independent process of synoecism? The answer is that it now seems reasonably certain that this process in Egypt did not take place without some direct influence from Mesopotamia. Recently Professor Edgerton of Chicago said: 'It seems to me as firmly established as any fact in early Egyptian history that important influences of many kinds reached Egypt from Mesopotamia just before the beginning of the First Dynasty.'[66]

Let us look at some of the archaeological evidence. Three Mesopotamian cylinder seals of the later Uruk or protoliterate period have been found in Egypt: one was from Naqada. From then onwards the Egyptians used the cylinder seal – a Mesopotamian invention [Plate 6] – and engraved these cylinder seals with their own traditional designs; they had no clay tablets and to them the seals were amulets. Then, secondly, Mesopotamian motifs appear in Egyptian art: these include hunting scenes, lions devouring cattle, beasts with long intertwined necks, serpopards, winged griffons, interlaced snakes. On the ivory handle of a flint knife from Gebel el-Arak, near Abydos, there is represented a Mesopotamian-type hero, rather resembling Gilgamesh, 'Lord of Beasts', subduing two lions [Plate 22], and the same theme is found on a wall-painting from Hierakonpolis, belonging to one of the earliest brick-built buildings in southern Egypt. On the back of the Gebel el-Arak knife [Plate 21] a water battle is represented in progress: in the upper row the boats have vertical prows and sterns which make them look like the *belems* of the Tigris; in the lower they are normal Egyptian boats of the period.[67]

In the third place, architecture. There appeared in Egypt a monumental style of building based on mud-brick, and we find the ancient Egyptians abandoning reeds, papyrus, palm branches and rush matting, and using sun-dried bricks made in wooden rectangular moulds. And in using bricks in their buildings they built recessed façades and pilasters such as were used in early buildings in Mesopotamia. And finally, writing. Hieroglyphic writing is first found on the slate palettes of late pre-dynastic times; it is already well advanced and is using ideograms and phonograms. This first Egyptian writing must surely be derived from the earlier Mesopotamian writing, but it is immediately different, as was the civilization that was dynastic Egypt.

What then had happened? There have been many explanations. Flinders Petrie saw the arrival of a new people from outside Egypt, Dr Baumgartel saw 'a fundamental and abrupt change'. This is not now the view of most scholars. Frankfort argued for a catalytic influence from Mesopotamia to Egypt, an influence of a selective, qualified and transient character which spurred on the synoecism that was about to happen and catalysed the process that was almost certainly going to happen anyway.[68] In a recent statement of the problem Cyril Aldred says it is difficult to deny that the early Egyptian peasant villages received something very considerable from outside, but not by conquest. He refers to 'the infiltration of new ideas and techniques', and says, 'What now permeated the native cultures were principles and ideas ... a foreign "know-how" was quickly seized upon and enthusiastically adapted to Egyptian conditions by a people ripe for change.'[69]

I would like to put it this way. The possibilities were there in a fertile river valley with a large population, and it has been estimated that late pre-dynastic Egypt had a population of between 100,000 and 200,000; and, moreover, a population that had to organize itself to deal with the irrigation problems of the annual Nile flood. The late pre-dynastic Egyptians were seizing these possibilities, but they were in contact with another river valley, Mesopotamia, which had achieved earlier the possibilities of synoecism. Some of the direct contacts that have been mentioned show that these Sumerian contacts hastened and effected the Egyptian development. I would suggest then that the origins of Egyptian civilization are to be explained in terms of stimulus diffusion from Sumeria to an essentially African society in the Nile Valley – a society which was already on its way to civilization, and might well have got there independently without benefit of Sumer.

We cannot of course be certain about these things and many Egyptologists are still unhappy about Frankfort's hypothesis of a catalytic influence of Sumer on Egypt, and do not like to think that Egyptian writing was in any way indebted to Sumerian cuneiform writing. What we can, however, be quite certain about is that, whatever may have been the manner in which the development from the later pre-dynastic societies to dynastic Egypt took place, Egyptian civilization – the creation of the men of the Nile Valley, however stimulated – was radically different from the Sumerian. It was Egyptian and it was African. In Sumer the ruler was a deputy of the gods, and was not himself divine. In Egypt the ruler was a god in his own person : he was not the human agent of the god – the Pharaoh is the classic example of the god incarnate as king. One could put it that he was the prehistoric African rain-maker chieftain become divine. The relation of the state to the law and the king-god was fundamentally different in Egypt from the situation in Sumer. Mesopotamia had, at a very early stage, efficient and effective written laws. In Egypt this was not so : rule was personal, and for two thousand five hundred years at least, Egypt was ruled by customary law – that is to say by the divine words of the god-king.

A second great difference was this : Egypt quickly became a nation-state without going through a period of city-states. When Egypt entered history and became civilized all the country from the Mediterranean to the First Cataract was one, and was under one ruler who ruled over a state six hundred miles long. This was the first state in history and was quite different from the cities of Sumer, which, eventually, became a nation under Agade. This difference serves to emphasize that what we are calling a civilization is a pattern, but the details of the pattern vary from one civilized society to another, and the final result always varies.

The cities of Sumer are obvious and clear for all to see, but where are the cities of ancient Egypt? When the Assyrians came to Egypt they spoke of hundreds of cities, but where are they now? Professor Wilson has called Egypt 'a civilization without cities': 'it is legitimate to say,' he writes, 'that for nearly three thousand years, until the founding of Alexandria, ancient Egypt was a major civilization without a single major city.'[70]

This is true to the extent that we cannot nowadays point to a great Egyptian prehistoric or protohistoric city and walk down its streets as we can walk down the streets of Mohenjo-daro and Harappa, for example. But I do not think it is legitimate or right to say that ancient Egypt was a civilization without cities. Professor Wilson is confusing what survives from the past with what existed in the past. Because none has survived, it does not follow that there were no ancient Egyptian cities, and it is not correct to characterize ancient Egyptian civilization as just an agricultural land full of villages. There were capitals – Memphis from 3000 B.C. and Thebes from about 2000 B.C. – and there were small towns like Heliopolis and Abydos. Many of the old Egyptian towns have been destroyed to build other and more modern towns: the Arab city of Cairo was built of stones from Memphis, and yet today Memphis is a *tell* which must cover the remains of an Old Kingdom town which should, some day, be excavated. Then again many of the Old Kingdom towns may be buried under modern towns or the Nile mud. Professor Butzer has drawn attention to the steady rise in the level of the Nile flood plain, and suggests that most of the important ancient sites may be covered with metres of silt. There are hundreds of pre-dynastic cemeteries from the more outlying areas of the Nile Valley, but the corresponding settlement sites are hardly known.[71]

What is certain is that in dynastic times very great works were undertaken which must indicate a complex and organized and surely urban life. The tombs of Dynasty I and II were single-storey structures. An early king of Dynasty III was Djoser: his Chancellor was Imhotep, a distinguished and versatile person later famed as architect, astronomer, priest, writer, and sage, and, above all, physician – he later became the Egyptian god of medicine. Imhotep planned a tomb for Djoser at Saqqara [Plate 15]: it was the first Pyramid – the Step Pyramid or the Step Mastaba as it is called. This was built in 2680 B.C. and was the wonder of the age: nothing like it had happened before. From this invention the huge pyramids of Giza developed. The great pyramid of King Kheops (Khufu) [Plates 16, 19] was built in the twenty-fifth century B.C.; two million large blocks of limestone were used in the construction of this tomb, and some of them weighed fifteen tons [Plates 17, 18]. This represents a fantastic piece of work and of organization: the figure of workmen supplied to Herodotus and repeated by him was a hundred thousand men, but others more recently have estimated that perhaps the figure was no more than 2,500. But whatever number of workmen we now allow, the grandeur and magnificence of this ancient Egyptian architecture remains. Even if the Sumerians were the first civilization, and even if it was their stimulus and example that catalysed the emergent or nascent synoecism of Egypt, the pyramids of the Nile Valley still pay silent and dramatic witness to the organization and power of the second civilization to develop in human history.

Let us now turn from the valley of the Nile to the valley of the Indus and the civilization that grew up and flourished there in the third and second millennia B.C. Before partition in 1947 it was easy to refer to this as the prehistoric civilization of India or of the Indian sub-continent. Now the sites of this civilization are divided between two nation states,

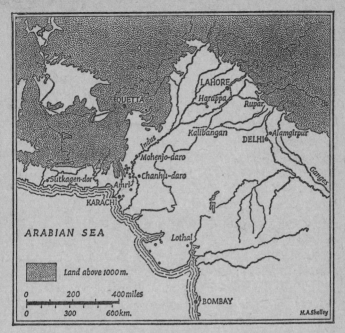

Figure 8. The Indus Valley, showing sites

namely Pakistan and India; the two main cities, Mohenjo-daro and Harappa [Plates 26–9], are now in Pakistan. Some writers prefer to call the civilization the Harappan after one of these cities, but I think the first and old nomenclature is the best and most convenient, and here we shall go on referring to the Indus civilization.

There was, until the early twenties, a traditional and generally accepted view of the remote Indian past. It was thought that the first cities were built in the first millennium B.C. by the descendants of pastoral nomads – the Aryans, who had come into India via the Khyber Pass from the north-west in the Bronze Age, and had introduced the language which developed into Sanskrit. It was thought that between say 1500 and 1000 B.C. they fought among themselves, and with the aborigines in the Punjab. Then it was supposed that they settled down and created the oldest Indian civilization in the basin of the Ganges, where the first, and therefore the holiest, city in India was Patna.

A word is necessary at this stage about the term Aryans – a word which got into considerable disrepute because of the excesses of Nazi racialists before and during the 1939–45 war. Sir William Jones, a Welshman educated at Oxford, who went out to be Chief Justice of the High Court in Calcutta in 1783, was the first British scholar to master Sanskrit. He realized to his surprise that there was an underlying relationship between Greek, Latin, Celtic, Persian and Sanskrit. The details of this underlying relationship were elaborated by later philologists and it became clear that there was a great language family having as its main branches Celtic, Italic, Hellenic, Slav, Teutonic and Indo-Persian. To this language family the name Indo-European or Indo-Germanic was given; by others the family was called Aryan. At the present day it is usually suggested that the whole language family should be referred to as Indo-European but that the branch of it which gave rise to the old languages of Persia and India can properly be referred to as Indo-Aryan or Aryan. The Sanskrit-speaking invaders of India did refer to themselves as the *aryas* or noble ones. Aryan is thus a linguistic term and by extension a term for the people who spoke this ancient language.[72]

Another point on which we must be clear is the proper connotation in writings on archaeology, anthropology and ancient history of words and concepts like race. The physical anthropologist means by race a group of people who have

1, 2. The tall mud-brick ziggurats of Mesopotamia are the basis of the legend of the Tower of Babel. *Plate* 1 is a view of the ziggurat of Ur, seen from the east before excavation; on the right of it is the steep ramp which led to the temple built on its top. *Plate* 2 is a view of the same ziggurat from the south-west, as seen today in its restored state

3. A detail of the mud-brick walls of the ziggurat at Ur. The apertures are 'weeper' holes which were designed to prevent the mud-brick core of the ziggurat from splitting when, during the rainy season, it became saturated with water

4. A small pillow-shaped limestone tablet from Kish, *c.* 3500 B.C. The pictographs, some of the oldest known picture writing, represent signs for a head, a foot and hand, a threshing sledge and numerals. *Ashmolean Museum, Oxford*

5. Clay foundation tablet of Eannatum, King of Lagash, *c.* 2500 B.C. It is written in the semi-pictographic Babylonian script and records the sinking of a well in the temple of the deity Ningirsu. *British Museum*

6. Impressions of three Babylonian cylinder seals. They represent: *above*, a king or captain with soldiers, one of whom to the left carries a bow and quiver of arrows; *centre*, a ritual scene with a winged god and kings; *below*, a bearded hero wearing a crown, possibly Gilgamesh, who grasps a pair of rampant bulls by their necks. *British Museum*

7. Seated statue in polished black stone of Gudea, who was King of Lagash in the late third millennium B.C. He is seen in the typical attitude of a servitor of the god, hands clasped meekly before him. The inscription on his skirt records his prayers to the gods for their benefactions. *Paris, Louvre*

8. Upper half of a diorite statue of Gudea, King of Lagash, or possibly his son Ur-Ningirsu from Telloh (Lagash). He stands in contemplation before the god (cf. *Plate* 7). The inscription has been effaced and partly broken away. *British Museum*

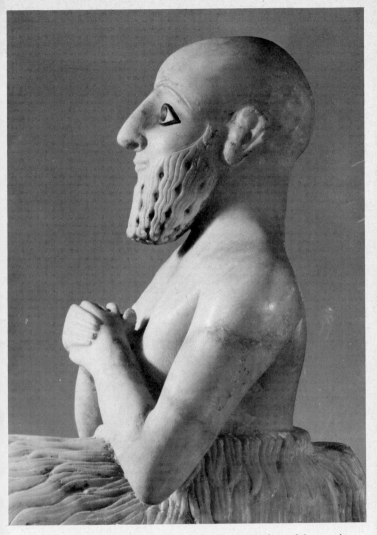

9. Seated alabaster statue of Ebikhil, who was Superintendent of the temple to the goddess Ishtar at Mari. His hands are clasped before him in the same attitude as Gudea (*Plate* 7) and he wears the typical Sumerian flounced skirt. *Damascus Museum*

10–13. The so-called 'Royal Standard of Ur', an oblong box decorated with figures of shell and limestone on a blue lapis-lazuli background, originally fastened with bitumen on to wood. It may possibly have been the sounding box of a harp. On one side are depicted scenes of war (10, 11), and on the other, scenes of peace (12, 13). Many of the objects illustrated, e.g. the rein ring on the back of the onagers in *Plate* 11, and the harp in the upper register in *Plate* 13, were found in the Royal Tombs at Ur. *British Museum*

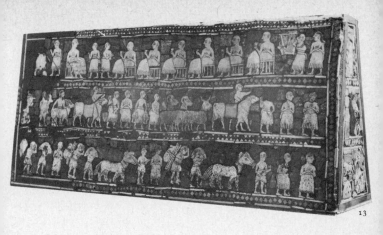

13

14. Engraving, published in 1846, of the famous trilingual inscription
carved on the vertical rock face at Behistun on the orders of Darius in 516 B.C.
It was this inscription which gave the Englishman Rawlinson the first clues
to the decipherment of the wedge-shaped cuneiform script

15, 16. The first stone-built monument was the Step Pyramid of King Djoser of Dynasty III, *above*, built at Saqqara for him by his architect Imhotep. The next dynasty, IV, saw the building of the great pyramids on the plateau at Giza, *right*. The earliest, one of the Seven Wonders of the Ancient World, was that of Kheops, seen here on the right, followed by the pyramids of his successors Khephren and Mykerinus. The small pyramids in the foreground are those of queens

17. A reconstruction of how the pyramids may have been built, using mud-brick ramps, gradually extended as the pyramid rose. This model shows the building of the pyramid of Mykerinus with the pyramid of Khephren in the background. *Boston, Massachusetts, Museum of Science*

18. A detail of the massive blocks, many weighing over twenty tons, used in the construction of the Great Pyramid of Kheops

19. View from the top of the Great Pyramid of Kheops, looking towards the area of cultivation and the Nile. The small pyramids in the foreground are those of queens and the 'streets' of mastabas behind them are the tombs of courtiers buried near their king. The oblong pit in the immediate foreground and that between two of the pyramids are boat pits, where actual boats were buried for the use of their owners in the after-world. Recently one such boat, intact, has been found at the south side of the Great Pyramid of Kheops

20. The slate palette, *right,* of Narmer, the first king of Dynasty I. The king is seen wearing the white crown (the *hedjet*) of Upper Egypt. He grasps an enemy by the forelock and is about to bring his mace down upon his head. Before him, the god Horus is seen assisting the king and holding a rope which runs from the nostrils of a prostrate enemy. Behind the king is his sandal-bearer and below his feet more vanquished enemies and a tiny representation of one of the towns which he has captured. *Cairo Museum*

21, 22. The Gebel el-Arak knife is one of the most famous of Egyptian antiquities from the Gerzean period. The blade of thin fine flint has been worked with the characteristic ripple-flaking technique.

Its handle is made of ivory and shows interesting Mesopotamian influences. On one side, *left,* a river battle is in progress; the ships have high prows and sterns, similar to boats found on the Tigris today. The other side, *above,* shows wild animals, lions, goats and most prominently a hero rather like the Mesopotamian Gilgamesh, subduing two lions (cf. *Plate* 6). *Paris, Louvre*

23. The Rosetta Stone, found by a French officer near the Rosetta mouth of the Nile. It bears a decree, dated to 196 B.C., with its text in Egyptian hieroglyphs, repeated in demotic (a later form of hieroglyphs) and Greek. It was the study of these three versions by the French scholar Champollion which led to the eventual decipherment of the ancient Egyptian script. *British Museum*

24. In a number of the tombs of courtiers at Saqqara and Giza of the Pyramid Age have been found statues of their owners represented as scribes, squatting with an open papyrus roll on their knees. Literacy in Ancient Egypt was restricted to the priests and upper classes. *Paris, Louvre*

25. Group statue of the dwarf Seneb with his wife and two children, a boy and girl. In the Old Kingdom, dwarfs often held high position, particularly as Keepers of the Treasury. The reason for this is summed up in the contemporary Egyptian saying, that they were most reliable in this office since they were unable to run very fast. The sculptor has overcome the difficulty of representing Seneb's stunted form with his normal wife and children in a very satisfactory manner. *Cairo Museum*

26, 27. Mohenjo-daro is one of the two classic cities of the Indus civilization. Today it is dominated by a Buddhist stupa, *above,* possibly on the site of an earlier citadel, overlooking the well-ordered streets and drainage system, *below*

28. A typical street in Mohenjo-daro. The walls in many instances
still stand today to their first-floor height. Windows are few and generally
the only large openings are the refuse chutes

29. The exact use to which the great bath at Mohenjo-daro, *above*, was put is not known, whether for secular or religious purposes. Measuring approximately 40 feet by 20 feet, it was made watertight with asphalt and at the south-west corner was drained by a high corbelled drain

30. The large dock at Lothal is a major feature of the site. In the foreground can be seen the top of a well-built sluice gate; the sides of the dock were revetted with brick

31. Seals of the Indus civilization show a wide variety of animals
and occasionally gods. *Top left,* possibly an early representation of the later
Indian god Siva. Among the animals seen here are bulls, the Indian humped
bull, elephants, water buffalo, and two curious beasts, one with three
heads and the other a 'unicorn' standing before an altar. *British Museum;
National Museum of Pakistan, Karachi*

32, 33. A tiny model cart, *left*, found at Mohenjo-daro, which bears a close resemblance to the bullock cart seen in the Punjab today, *right*

34-6. Numerous terracotta figurines have been found at the major Indus Valley sites. Here are shown a bull, a very grotesque figure of a woman seen in front view and profile, and a second figure of a woman loaded with jewellery, wearing a curious high plumed headdress. *National Museum of Pakistan, Karachi*

37. Stone sculpture in the Indus civilization is rare. One of the finest is this figure of a 'priest-king' or god from Mohenjo-daro. He is characterized by narrow slit eyes and a receding forehead; the fillet around his head has a small ring in the centre, seen again on his armlet. The remains of his cloak are decorated with a trefoil pattern. *National Museum of Pakistan, Karachi*

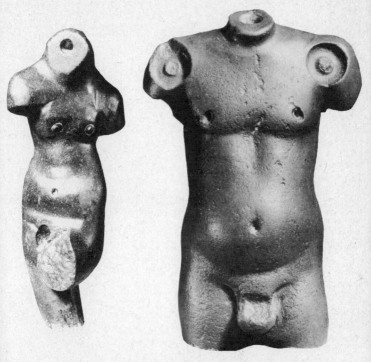

38, 39. Two torsos from Harappa, reproduced approximately actual size. One, *left,* is of red stone, the other, *right,* of grey stone. Note the high degree of modelling and the sophisticated technique of the head and arms being made separately to fit into sockets. *National Museum, New Delhi*

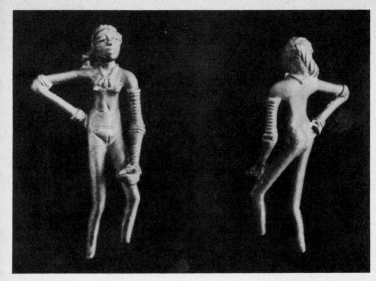

40, 41. Such bronzes as have survived from
Indus Valley sites are mostly in very poor condition.
One of the finest is the little dancing girl, *above,*
from Mohenjo-daro. She is naked save for her
necklace and many bangles. Her long hair is drawn
back, and the tilt of her head and expression in
the face, together with the easy attitude in which
she stands, give her a most provocative air.
Right, another small bronze figurine from
Mohenjo-daro which has its arm in much the same
attitude with hand on hip. By comparison,
however, this figurine is completely lifeless.
National Museum, New Delhi

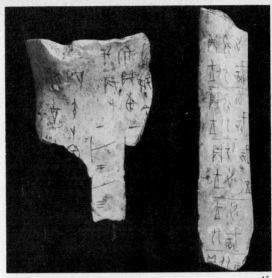

42

42-5. Fortune-telling and divination played a highly important role in early China. Often a question to be put to the oracle would be inscribed upon a scrap of bone (42, 43); an answer could be obtained by placing a red-hot piece of metal against the bone (44), and the resultant cracks which appeared on the opposite side (45) read to give a suitable pronouncement. *British Museum*

43   44   45

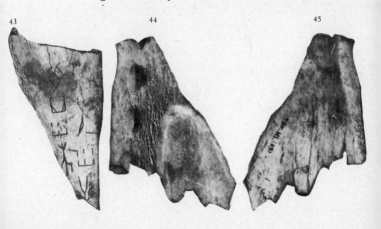

46. A bronze ritual vessel, *tsun*, of the Shang dynasty, in the shape of an elephant. A number of burials of complete elephants have been excavated near Anyang, the Shang capital

47. Fine engraving and a sense of humour are a feature of this elephant-shaped Shang ritual vessel. The tiny elephant on its parent's back adopts an identical attitude. *Freer Gallery of Art, Washington, D.C.*

48. Shang metalworkers delighted in their craft, as may be seen in the exuberance of some of the forms taken by their ritual vessels. This example is a wine vessel, *yu*, in the shape of a very stylized owl. *British Museum*

49. A Shang bronze ritual vessel, *tsun*, which has been cast in the shape of two addorsed rams

50. A view of the central pit of a Shang tomb, excavated at Wu Kuan Ts'un, near the Shang capital of Anyang. On the ledge around the central pit may be seen the skeletons of human, sacrificed, funeral victims

51. Charioteers with their chariot and horses are often found buried on the entrance ramps to the great Shang tombs. Though the wooden chariot has perished, the recesses which once held the shaft, axle and lower parts of the wheels are clearly visible

52. This bronze tripod ritual vessel of the Shang period is decorated over-all with a very stylized version of the *t'ao t'ieh* mask. This curious monster mask is a wholly Chinese invention, often found on bronzes and occasionally on pottery

53. A bronze *chia* used for warming black millet wine. Its shape and style place it in the early Shang period. *British Museum*

54. The complex over-all and highly ornamented decoration is a feature of this bronze *fang-yi*, a ritual food container (Chou style). Bird motifs appear on the panels at the base but the major part of the decoration consists of the *t'ao t'ieh* monster mask (cf. *Plate* 52). *Freer Gallery of Art, Washington, D.C.*

55. A rare example of Shang sculpture, this seated figure of a man in limestone is the only known piece representing a person. It was excavated at SSŭ P'an Mo, near the Shang capital, Anyang

56. One of the most remarkable bronze pieces to survive from pre-Han China is this group representing two wrestlers, or possibly acrobats, of the fifth to fourth century B.C. They were presumably buried with and intended for the entertainment of the deceased in the after-world. *British Museum*

57. A curious feature of a number of Olmec sites are colossal basalt heads, measuring up to 9 feet in height. Some wear a frown and a helmet, others, as this one from Huimanguille, La Venta, an enigmatic twisted grin. The expression on their faces is seen even in miniature Olmec work such as jades (cf. *Plates* 60–62)

58. A hollow pottery figurine of a baby found at Tlatilco. It has a typically Olmec face

59. The so-called 'Wrestler', a basalt figure of a bearded man of the Olmec culture

60. Small jade effigy of a 'were-jaguar', of the Olmec culture. The carving of the face with heavy brows and wide mouth, in conjunction with the delicately engraved details on the body, are characteristic of Olmec work. *British Museum*

61. This standing figure of green jade, a material much used by the Olmecs, carries another small figure in front of it. The faces of both of them exhibit the drooping mouth and elongated eyes which are so very typical of this culture (cf. *Plates* 58, 60, 62). *Brooklyn Museum*

62. A cache found at the Olmec centre of La Venta. The sixteen small figurines of jade and serpentine, none taller than eight inches, together with the six jade axeheads, are seen *in situ*, obviously arranged to form some kind of ritual scene

63. Carved basalt monolith from La Venta. It represents a figure wearing a jaguar headdress, seated within the curve of a plumed rattlesnake

64. The city of Teotihuacán was laid out on a grid pattern, and the field boundaries seen in this air view correspond roughly to old foundation walls. In the centre is the Pyramid of the Sun and in the left foreground, the Pyramid of the Moon. They are connected by the Avenue of the Dead

65. One of the dominant monuments at Chichen Itzá, Yucatán, is the temple of Kukulkan, often referred to as 'El Castillo'. A flight of steep steps on each side gives access to the temple which crowns its summit

66. A view from the north end of the main plaza at Monte Albán.
Most of the buildings to be seen date from *c.* 100 B.C. to *c.* A.D. 950, a later
stage in the development of the site. An earlier period, Stage II *c.* 350–100 B.C.,
is represented by the building just behind the central pyramid

67. Detail of a carved
stone revetment slab from
a group in the south-west
corner of the main plaza
at Monte Albán. The
figures, in low relief, are
known as 'Los Danzantes'
(dancers); there are in all
some 140 figures, dating
from Stage I, *c.* 800–350 B.C.

68. A view of Machu Picchu, the 'lost city' of the Incas high in the Andes, found by the American explorer Hiram Bingham in 1912, as it was when abandoned on the arrival of the Spaniards some 400 years ago. Although difficult of access, modern transport has now made the site a favourite tourist centre

69. A gold pendant from a Mixtec burial in Tomb 7 at Monte Albán.
It shows a head surmounted by a rich headdress issuing from a pair of plaques.
These plaques carry Mixtec year symbols

70. A Mixtec gold buckle ornament from Monte Albán. It represents the flayed god Xipe with closed eyes, a ring through his nose, a stud in his upper lip, and heavy circular earrings. *National Museum of Anthropology, Mexico City*

71-3. Much of the pottery from Peru takes on fantastic zoomorphic or anthropomorphic shapes. These three examples of stirrup jars show: *right,* two monkeys clinging to the belly of the jar; *below left,* a seated man beating a drum with a stick; *below right,* a Mochica vase representing a water fowl sitting on its nest in the reeds. 73, *British Museum*

74, 75. Animals apparently scaling the sides of a vessel and thus acting as handles are a favourite Inca motif. It is here used on a pottery vessel, *above,* and a basalt bowl, *below.* Motifs on the pot consist of jaguars and snakes and on the bowl of an indeterminate four-legged creature with a long tail. *Museum of Archaeology, Cuzco*

76. A stone lintel from Yaxchilán, Guatemala, showing a devotee kneeling before a priest. The devotee is drawing a cord studded with thorns through his tongue and the blood falls into a small basket at the priest's feet, ready to be offered. Late Classic Maya *c.* A.D. 750. *British Museum*

77. Reclining stone figures with a bowl (probably for offerings) resting on the stomach are known as Chac-Mools. They were set up before the entrance to an Aztec temple. This example is now in the courtyard of the National Museum of Anthropology, Mexico City

78. Aztec temples were built at the top of a pyramid and were the scene of human sacrifices to the Aztec god. The pottery model, *right,* representing one of these pyramids, is now in the University Museum of Archaeology and Ethnography, Cambridge

inherited heritable physical characteristics in common: it is essentially a biological term, and the races of men are like the breeds of cats and dogs – the French word for animal breeds is *race* – with of course this difference, that the various breeds of cats and dogs and other animals in captivity have been organized by selective breeding, whereas the physical varieties of man have come about, for the greater part, naturally. Perhaps saying that a race is a group of people with physical characteristics in common may give rise to the idea that it is a group living in one and the same place. This is not so, but it must have been true for the periods when these physical breeds of man crystallized out and were stabilized as types. Once they had become stable and recognizable human variants, however, the development of contacts and the increase of movement with modern civilization caused great intermixture of these types, so that racial heritages became confused and the existence of 'pure' races more difficult to isolate. Nevertheless, those racial heritages are there still, and the physical variants of the human species – for the phrase 'the human race' is a misnomer – are with us for all to see. Even the most violent anti-classifier of races, the person who insists perversely that races do not exist any more, would have as little difficulty in distinguishing an Eskimo from a Bushman as we have in distinguishing a tail-less Pembrokeshire Corgi from a Pyrenean mountain dog. Ask any cartoonist to draw delegates at an international conference and he will have no difficulty in distinguishing Chinese from Mediterraneans and both from Hottentots and Nordics.[73]

It is clear, then, that race – exemplified by the physical differences that exist between different breeds of men – can have nothing to do with the origins of civilization. The Sumerians and the Egyptians are physically dissimilar; and the folk of the Indus civilization were different from both Sumerians and Egyptians [Plates 37–41]. We shall see in the next few chapters that the creators of the early civilizations of China and Mesoamerica differed in physical type from those who created the first three Old World civilizations. It must also be clear that the Aryans were not a racial group. The Nazi propagandists and others before and after them have left a confusion in the mind of many that the Aryans were Nordics, but this they certainly were not. You must not therefore imagine hordes of fair-haired blue-eyed tall Nordics such as we find nowadays more frequently in Scandinavia than in other parts of Europe, pouring into India via the Khyber Pass between 1500 and 1200 B.C., introducing a language which subsequently became Sanskrit; though no doubt there were fair elements in this new population. The point is that they called themselves *aryas,* so that the term Aryan is very properly used for these people as a whole.

The sacred hymns of the *aryas* were transmitted orally and were not written down until the eighteenth century A.D. They contain references to the aborigines or indigenous population in India whom they confronted as conquerors: they called them the *Dasus* or *Dasyus* and described them as small, dark-skinned and flat-faced. The *Dasus* did not speak an Aryan language and were described as 'hostile-speaking' by their conquerors who regarded them with a mixture of contempt and fear – creatures to be either exterminated or enslaved. Indeed *Dasi* became the word for a female slave. All this might well be thought to be the standard description of a conquering people for the natives they were overpowering and enslaving, but there were one or two very unusual things in the description of the *Dasus:* they were said to live in great and wealthy cities and in addition to be skilled in various arts.

These were curious statements which few people gave much credence to; among those who did was Bishop Caldwell, who argued that the pre-Aryan Dravidians possessed temples, cities, metal instruments and written books – in fact that they were civilized.[74] These pre-Aryan cities were rediscovered in the twenties of the present century. In 1913 Barrett, beginning his book on *The Antiquities of India* with the Sanskrit hymn, the Rig-Veda, had maintained: 'In India there is no twilight before the dark.' The first volume of the *Cambridge History of India* was published in 1922 and in it Sir John Marshall, then Director-General of Archaeology in India, was still able to write: 'It is the misfortune of Indian history that its earliest and most obscure pages derive little light from contemporary antiques.'[75] Yet two years later he was announcing in the *Illustrated London News* the excavations of 1921 at Harappa and Mohenjo-daro [Plates 26–9], and the discovery of the prehistoric Indus civilization.

Years of work in the twenties and thirties built up a picture of the Indus civilization. Towards the end of the 1939–45 war Sir Mortimer Wheeler became Director General of Archaeology in India, and restarted work at the Indus cities and other allied sites, which has very considerably changed our views about them. Since partition, work has been going on in Pakistan and in India and our knowledge of the Indus civilization grows steadily from year to year.[76]

We now realize that it was very extensive geographically and spread over an area much larger than either early dynastic Egypt or Sumer. From north to south the Indus civilization extends a thousand miles, and geographically it is the largest of the four ancient civilizations known to us in the Old World. It is still best known from its two main cities, Mohenjo-daro beside the River Indus in Sind some 140 miles north-east of Karachi, and Harappa beside a former course of the Ravi nearly 400 miles north-east. Other interesting and important sites are Amri, dug in 1929, Chanhu-daro and Kot Diji, twenty-five miles east of Mohenjo-daro, and the new sites of Kalibangan in Rajasthan and Lothal in Gujerat [Plate 30] – the latter site being a port. Both Mohenjo-daro and Harappa are cities upwards of three miles in circuit. They have citadels and ceremonial centres [Plate 26] – the same formula as for the Sumerian cities although the detail is quite different, as is the character of the cities themselves. These two Indus cities have their main streets laid out on a grid-iron plan: and this rectangular town-planning is a 'first' in human history that cannot be claimed by Sumer. And many of the houses are organized as flats, and are equipped with rubbish bins, and the streets have brick-built drains [Plate 27].

The Indus civilization, like the civilizations of Sumer and Egypt, was based on agriculture – wheat, six-rowed barley, field peas, melons, sesame, dates and cotton, the earliest cotton in the world; the domestic animals were cattle [Plates 32–3], camels, buffaloes, asses and horses. There was of course specialization among the workers in the cities, who included many skilled craftsmen, particularly those making seals [Plate 31]. It is on the seals that the Indus pictographic writing is best found, a writing that has not yet been deciphered. The people of the Indus civilization had extensive trade relations with Afghanistan, Iran, Mesopotamia, and south India. The relations with Mesopotamia are well attested and quite clear. In the time of Sargon of Akkad, whose date is now generally accepted as around 2350 B.C., various objects reached the Mesopotamian cities from the Indus Valley probably via Bahrain and the Persian Gulf – the Dilmun of the ancients. These were pottery, seals, beads and small objects [Plates 34–6], and it is important to emphasize that these objects were small. As Wheeler has said: 'The Indus civilization provides a clear, though not the only, instance of an interchange of ornaments and charms combined with a basic technological independence.'[77]

Now let us address ourselves to the problem of the origins of the Indus civilization. What was its origin, this civilization so different from that of the Sumerians and the Egyptians and yet so similar in essentials – a civilization based on a prosperous agriculture in a fertile river valley full of possibilities and full of dangers and hazards, a civilization with large organized towns housing specialized and expert craftsmen, with central ceremonial centres, and with wide trading relations?

There have been, naturally enough, many suggestions. The first was that the Indus civilization was a colonial off-shoot of one of the other two civilizations – Sumer and Egypt – both of which were certainly earlier in date. This theory is chronologically possible; early Sumer and early dynastic Egypt almost certainly precede the Indus cities by at least half a millennium, and, possibly, in the case of Sumer, by a millennium. Elliott Smith and Perry regarded the Indus civilization as an offshoot of Egypt, Lord Raglan of Sumer. At the present day it seems that neither is a possible hypothesis. Sir Mortimer Wheeler has said: 'Basic differences . . . between the Indus and Mesopotamian civilization bar the possibility of any direct colonization of the former from the latter.'[78] I think this is very true, but in agreeing with this, we must remember that the differences between the Indus and the Sumerian civilization are differences in the detailed performance of basic concurrences. There are basic parallels of great importance – the attributes of the city itself, widespread trade, flourishing and well-organized agriculture, specialist crafts, ceremonial centres.

Figure 9. The Indus Valley and Persian Gulf, showing distribution of seals

There are without doubt basic likenesses between the patterns of civilization that emerged in proto-historic times on the banks of the Tigris-Euphrates, Nile and Indus. The questions we must ask ourselves are: Why is the pattern so different in detail? What are the interrelations of the three patterns?

The second view of the origin of the Indus civilization is that it arose independently in north-western India out of the village cultures that existed there in the early third millennium. This view would see prosperous peasant village economies in a rich land as leading – not perhaps leading inevitably, but having the possibility of leading – to rich and varied urban economies. To put it another way, synoecism could happen as a natural possible process of human social evolution in the Indus Valley as it did in Mesopotamia and on the Nile, and was later to do in Greece: that is to say that Childe's Urban Revolution repeated itself in several places at several different times.

Sir Mortimer Wheeler, who has done more than most to re-study the Indus civilization in the last quarter century and who has faced squarely, and with full knowledge and appreciation of the archaeological facts, the problems of the origins of this civilization, propounds a view which is a third and separate point of view. He agrees that the Indus civilization could not have been a colonial outpost of Sumer, and equally he cannot see it originating absolutely independently in north-western India. Let us quote his views:

A society determined to profit by the vast opportunities of the plain must needs have also the genius and the skill to master an exciting and minatory environment, *and must have it from the outset*. A civilization such as that of the Indus cannot be visualized as a slow and patient growth. Its victories, like its problems, must have been of a sudden sort: and our search therefore for a systematic material ancestry for the Indus civilization may well be a long and subtle and perhaps not primarily important one. Intellectually, the founders of that civilization had one crowning advantage. Two great riverine civilizations had shortly preceded them, in Mesopotamia and Egypt. In any physical sense, neither of these was the immediate parent: the Indus civilization, with its individual technology and script and its alien personality, was no mere colony of the West. But ideas have wings, and in the third millennium the *idea* of civilization was in the air in western Asia. A model of civilization, however abstract, was present to the minds of the Indus founders. In their running battle against more spacious problems than had been encountered either in Mesopotamia or in Egypt, they were fortified by the consciousness that *it had been done before*. And in that consciousness, after one failure and another (Amri and Kot Diji are merely examples) they won through. In some such manner may be reconstructed the initial phase of the Indus Civilization, as the ultimate triumph of a village or small-town community, determined, well led and inspired by a great and mature idea. The Indus people were neither the first nor the last to fulfil themselves in this dramatic fashion; and it is a fashion not easy to reconstruct on the limited basis of conventional archaeological evidence. It is not necessarily the less objectively true for that disability, for the abstract element in its composition.[79]

That is what Sir Mortimer Wheeler wrote and the phrases in italics are italicized by him. I have quoted this passage at length because it is the most thoughtful account of the difficult problems of understanding the origins of a civilization. We can in fairness call this third view of the origin of the Indus civilization that of idea diffusion: peoples who were peasant villagers got the idea of civilization from Sumer, from an area where it had been done before, and determined to do the same in the Indus Plain.

I think I am nearly with Wheeler in his views but sufficiently far off to put forward a fourth view, although in the end it might be thought to be no more than a modification of the Wheeler idea-diffusion view. It is quite clear to me that the Indus civilization was no colony of Sumer or Egypt and equally clear that it did not develop in complete isolation. Its origin, like the origin of Egyptian civilization, was due to stimulus-diffusion from the Sumerians. I see the process as having happened in this way: fairly advanced village communities in north-western India were in contact through the Persian Gulf with Sumer in the middle of the third millennium B.C. There was already in those villages the possibility of synoecism, and these possibilities may have been temporarily and unsuccessfully exploited at places like Amri and Kot Diji. They were, however, successfully exploited in the area from Mohenjo-daro to Harappa by people inspired by the achievements of the Sumerians in a similar geographical and socio-cultural environment. Ideas may have wings, but no more than battle-axes or the technique of *cire-perdue* casting can they travel without men. It was the men from the growing north-west Indian villages who came back from their journeys to Sumer, their ships docking at Dilmun on the way to Lothal, that brought back an idea, and not to my mind the idea of civilization, but rather the vision of Mesopotamia, the knowledge that villages could be grouped together and grow into towns and cities, and that an urban literate life could be created if you worked hard and planned hard and knew what was to happen.

The realization of the existing possibilities of synoecism, together with the stimulus of Sumer, produced a civilization in India which was, as we have said, in its basic elements identical with those of Sumer and Egypt, but in its detailed manifestations quite different. The pattern is the same, because it is the pattern of civilization, but the quilt that was woven out of that basic pattern varied in its colours in each of the three ancient river valleys we have been discussing. We will find in the next chapter when we discuss the fourth of the first civilizations of the Old World that, though the same pattern is present in China, the colours there, too, are different.

CHAPTER FIVE

CHINA: THE YELLOW RIVER CIVILIZATION

In the previous three chapters we have been dealing with the three ancient riverine civilizations of Mesopotamia, Egypt and the Indus Valley. We now turn to the fourth of the ancient riverine civilizations of the Old World, that of the Yellow River in China.

I have already said that most of us from our schooldays, and Sunday-school days, think that we know something about the ancient Egyptians, although what we actually knew about them was little and what we knew of their origins was even less. That mythical person, the general reader, has inherited some mystique about ancient Egypt; in the same way we have all inherited some kind of mystique about China. China, most people think, was indeed an ancient civilization which invented gunpowder and paper-making; a civilization which was ancient when Marco Polo and Friar Rubuck visited it in the thirteenth century A.D. Before the discoveries of archaeology no one probably was prepared to consider the existence of early civilizations in Mesopotamia and the Indian sub-continent, or for that matter, Crete. But there was, before ever archaeology began to illuminate the Chinese past, an idea that culture – high culture and that complicated form of high culture we call civilization – had a great antiquity in China, as it did in Egypt. The Jesuit missionaries did transmit to Europe in the eighteenth century a picture of a very ancient China which went back to the third millennium B.C.

This idea of the great antiquity of China is only one of the many attitudes which the western world has adopted towards China in the last thousand years. These attitudes have recently been summarized with great percipience, wit and wisdom by Raymond Dawson in an essay entitled 'Western Conceptions of Chinese Civilization'. Dawson is a Lecturer in Chinese in the University of Oxford and his essay forms the first chapter in a book, *The Legacy of China*, edited by Dawson himself.[80] In this essay he lists the various Western conceptions, or perhaps one should say misconceptions, of China that have at various times flourished. 'China the Ancient' I have already mentioned. Another view was that of China as a land of great material prosperity, a view which was due much to Marco Polo and the other travellers of the thirteenth century. Marco Polo loved exaggeration – he was not nicknamed *Il Milione* for nothing – and one remembers his famous description of Hangchow with its 'Twelve thousand bridges of stone, for the most part so lofty that a great fleet could pass beneath them', and his statement that at the New Year, the Great Khan customarily received 'a hundred thousand white horses richly caparisoned'.

This sinophile attitude, this myth of the rich China with its wholesome climate and its happy hard-working peasants and its fabulous prosperity, survived into the late eighteenth century. In his *First Essay on Population*, published in 1798, Malthus declared that China was the richest country in the world, and in the previous year Sir George Staunton wrote: 'In respect to its natural and artificial productions, the policy and uniformity of its government, the language, manners and opinions of the people, their moral maxims and civil institutions, and the general economy and tranquillity of the state, it is the grandest collective object that can be presented for human contemplation and research.'[81] Incidentally, when the embassy led by Earl Macartney went to Peking at the close of the eighteenth century to try to establish more satisfactory commercial arrangements with the Chinese, they could not find a single Englishman who knew anything at all of the Chinese language, so that, in the words of John Francis Davis, they 'were somewhat discreditably reduced to the necessity of engaging the services of two Romish priests to aid in the important objects of the mission in the quality of interpreters.'[82] Clearly love and admiration for China did not extend to reading and speaking Chinese.

The picture of China as part of an opulent Orient changed in the quarter century following Malthus's *Essay* and Staunton's account of the Macartney Embassy. Protestant missionaries took a jaundiced view of China: it was 'a second class country peopled by those who, lacking the light of God, must inevitably be regarded as inferior beings'.[83] But this view had existed earlier. In 1719 Defoe made Robinson Crusoe say, 'I must confess it seemed strange to me, when I came home, and heard our people say such fine things of the power, glory and magnificence and trade of the Chinese; because as far as I saw, they appeared to be a contemptible herd or crowd of ignorant, sordid savages, subjected to a government qualified only to rule such people.'

These fascinating misconceptions of Chinese civilization were those propagated by missionaries and travellers, as so frequently missionaries and travellers, consciously and unconsciously, propagate misconceptions. Professional historians and archaeologists have, as professional historians and archaeologists from time to time, consciously or unconsciously, do, propagated other misconceptions. One was that China was changeless, and has always been changeless.

Leopold von Tanke, in his *Weltgeschichte* (Leipzig, 1881), said that China was in a state of 'eternal standstill', and Oliver Goldsmith in his *The Citizen of the World* (London, 1762), called China 'an Empire which has continued invariably the same for such a long succession of ages'. 'We have before us,' wrote Hegel, 'the oldest state and yet no past, but a state which exists today as we know it to have been in ancient times. To that extent China has no history.' Condorcet believed the same but did not approve: he talked of the 'shameful stagnation in those vast empires whose uninterrupted existence has dishonoured Asia for so long'.[84]

The second scholarly misconception was that of the great antiquity of China, and De Quincey provides a good example of this view. 'The mere antiquity of Asiatic things,' he wrote, 'of their institutions, histories, modes of faith, etc., is so impressive that to me the vast age of the race and name overpowers the sense of youth in the individual. A young Chinese seems to me an antediluvian man renewed!' I think many people still share the notion of the great antiquity of China and the great ancientness of Chinese civilization, and many are among those whom Raymond Dawson castigates as believing the name China to be 'still mainly associated with such trivialities as pigtails, slant eyes, lanterns, laundries, pidgin English, chopsticks and bird's-nest soup . . . a quaint civilization which resembles the design on a willow-pattern plate'.[85]

Let us now turn to the view of their past held by the Chinese themselves. The traditional historical picture of China in pre-archaeological days was all worked out from myths, legends and pseudo-histories. First, of course, was the creation of the universe, often attributed to P'an-ku, its catastrophic destruction by a great deluge, its reconstruction by Nu-wa, who is sometimes accredited with creating human beings. Later there came legendary monarchs and cultural heroes, sometimes organized in a scheme called that of the Three Sovereigns and the Five Emperors, who invented dwellings, fire, agriculture, writing, and social and political institutions. Then this was followed by the Three Dynasties called Hsia, Shang, and Chou which were considered to initiate the historical period. The philosophy of Confucius, who died in 479 B.C., insisted that China was always ruled by emperors and always subject to a single ruler. There were some pre-Hsia rulers beginning with T'ai Hao, who was said to have occupied the throne from 2852 B.C. It is possible to discredit all or much of this, but some of this is clearly legend and not myth, and some is near-history.[86]

What cannot be discredited is that in A.D. 52 Yüan K'ang published a book entitled *Yüeh Chüeh Shu*, and in the chapter on Swords quotes an Eastern Chou philosopher, by name Feng Hu Tzu, as saying to a king of Yüeh that:

In the age of the Hsüan-yüan, Shen-nung and Hê-hs, weapons were made of stones for cutting trees and building houses, and were buried with the dead.... In the age of Huang-ti, weapons were made of jade, for cutting trees, building houses and digging the ground ... and were buried with the dead. In the age of Yü, weapons were made of bronze for building canals ... and houses. At the present time, weapons are made of iron.

This remarkable passage is very much an anticipation of the Three-Age system of Thomsen, and the Four-Age system of Lubbock with its Palaeolithic, Neolithic, Bronze and Iron Ages.[87]

So it is clear that the Chinese themselves had, as a legendary kind of ancient history, some awareness of the technological development through which their ancestors had passed. Let us now turn to what archaeology says about their origins, for it is only archaeology that in the past half-century has revealed to us the early civilization of China. The Greeks and Romans had of course got to China but they no more brought back to the western world knowledge of the beginnings of Chinese civilization than did the Greeks at Taxila bring back to the west knowledge of the beginnings of the civilization of India and Pakistan in the Indus Valley. Anyang, like Mohenjo-daro and Harappa, was buried in the earth and the revelation of its testimony, like theirs, awaited the spade. The first western contacts with India and China were with later proto-historic and historic empires, not with the first civilizations.[88]

In the centuries following Alexander the Great a vast empire was created in India: Chandragupta ruled from Kabul to Bengal, and his grandson Asoka who reigned from 269 to 232 B.C. ruled over what was virtually the whole of the sub-continent. In China the Ch'in dynasty, established in 221 B.C., covered the whole territory from the Great Wall down to Tongking; and let us not forget the size of China. It is, like India, a sub-continent, with an area of 3·7 million square miles, about a quarter as large again as the United States of America. Hidden in a small part of these great Asian empires were the homelands of two early civilizations. In India the homeland was in the basin of the River Indus, and in China it was in the basin of the Yellow River. The first agriculturists in China and later the first civilization arose in the region extending westwards from the coast approximately between the 35th and 40th parallels of latitude; that is to say, the lower and middle courses of the Yellow River as far as its abrupt northward turn on the boundary of Shensi province.

Until 1920, though there was in some quarters a vague and

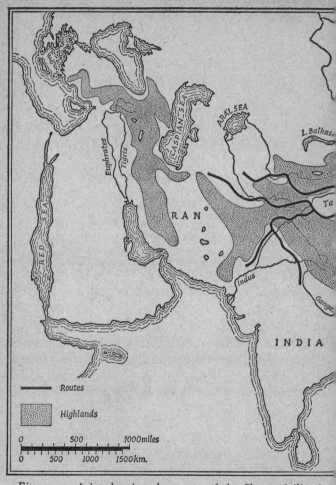

Figure 10. Asia, showing the centre of the Shang civilization
and routes to and from the West [after Gernet]

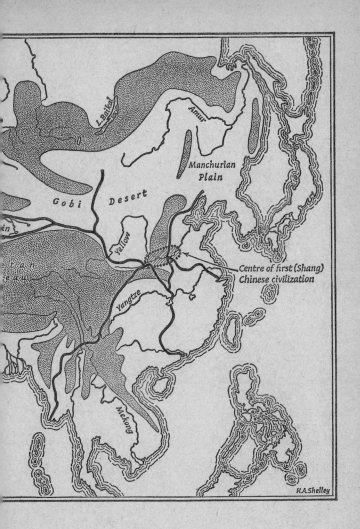

Gobi   Desert

L. Baikal

Amur

Manchurian
Plain

Yellow

Yangtze

Centre of first (Shang)
Chinese civilization

Mekong

H.A.Shelley

general appreciation of the antiquity of ancient Chinese civilization, and, as we have seen, much misconception about China, it was thought that China had no prehistory. In his *Prehistoric Man*, published in 1925, the French archaeologist Jacques de Morgan declared that 'Chinese civilization dates from the seventh or eighth centuries B.C.; we are completely ignorant of its prehistory.' In 1920, when H. G. Wells produced his *Outline of History*, a most remarkable and interesting work, there was nothing in it about early Chinese civilization, and Berthold Laufer, in his *Jade: A Study in Chinese Archaeology and Religion* (1922), said that Chinese civilization had no prehistory.

In 1921 a Swede, John Gunnar Andersson, identified the first Neolithic peasant village community in China from a site which he excavated at Yang Shao in Honan, and from that time onwards more villages of this Yang Shao culture have been found. The distribution of these sites in China is widespread and the total area of the Yang Shao culture is equal to that of the cultures of ancient Egypt or Mesopotamia. These first Chinese villagers had wheat, but their main grain was millet. How far rice entered into the economy of the Yang Shao people we do not know: there are rice-grain impressions on a potsherd unearthed by Andersson. The Yang Shao villagers had pigs, cattle, sheep, dogs, chickens, and, possibly, horses. Their villages were undefended or lightly defended, and were built just above the flood plain to avoid seasonal flooding. They kept domesticated silk-worms and had looms: their clothes were of silk and of hemp. They made pots, some coarse, some of fine quality, and the fine pots were painted.[89]

The earliest date for the Yang Shao villages seems to be somewhere in the middle or at the end of the third millennium B.C. This is of course very much later than the date of incipient agriculture and the date of the first settled peasant farmers in the ancient Near East, the south-west of Asia: here there were farmers and potters six thousand years before Yang Shao. We cannot rule out the possibility that the Yang Shao farmers were a distant eastern outpost of the early peasant-village economy of south-west Asia. Neolithic farmers could have travelled along the central Asian routes which were later used by the Greeks and by the travellers of the Middle Ages. The silk-route could have been pioneered in the third millennium B.C.[90]

From time to time some parallels between certain aspects of the Chinese Neolithic and the Neolithic of the west have been listed. There are parallels between the designs on some Yang-shao pots and pots from Susa in Iran; and the large urns from Pan Shan in Kansu have, without doubt, a general resemblance to the painted jars from Tripolye, from Trialeti during the Caucasian Bronze Age, and Anau in Turkestan. Then it has been argued that the wheat, cattle and sheep found in the Chinese Neolithic communities must come from the Near East. On the strength of this, and because the model of prehistorical thought in the twenties and thirties was basically a diffusionist one, an invasion hypothesis was built up which brought the first Chinese peasant-farmers from the Near East. Childe argued for this, but Andersson was not impressed.[91]

By now opinion on this matter has changed very considerably. Watson says roundly that 'there can be no question of a complete transfer of any culture to China from the Far West'. K. C. Chang expresses an even firmer view when he says that 'practically all archaeologists would unhesitatingly rule out the first alternative on the basis of the available materials', and here the first alternative is the western origin of Chinese village farming. Chang argues strongly for the local origin of incipient agriculture in northern China, and its gradual local development into the Yang Shao villages, and, viewing the whole problem of agricultural origins in the Old World, he sees two original centres of farming, one in the Iraq-Iran-Turkey area, and the other in the Hwang-Ho. Chang sees the spread of farming as happening from these two centres along the intervening steppe zone and from opposite directions, of course, and concludes that there would naturally be scattered contacts. That, he argues, would explain the resemblances in the painted pottery, and could also be responsible for the spread of wheat, sheep and cattle from the West to the East. This again would be an example of stimulus-diffusion, of the diffusion of ideas, of actual knowledge, and of certain cultural traits, without the mass migration of people. It seems to me that this view set out by Chang is right, and that the increasingly widely held view of the independent origin of Chinese agriculture is also right.

But at the moment we are still discussing the peasant villages which, as in Mesopotamia and Egypt and India, lay behind the earliest Chinese civilization. Let us now turn to the archaeology of these first Chinese cities. During the last few decades of the nineteenth century, farmers tilling the fields near the tiny village of Hsiao T'un near Anyang in north Honan – right in the northern tip of this province – found curious bits of bone, some of which were decorated with characters [Plates 42–5]. It was in a locality traditionally called Yin Hsu, or the waste of Yin: and Yin is another form of the name Shang. These curious bits of bone with their inscribed characters were ground up by Chinese apothecaries for use as medicine. They were recognized to be oracle-bones of the Shang or Yin dynasty. A word about oracle-bones. They are used, as the name suggests, for the purpose of augury, and this method, using bones, has survived until very recently among Mongol tribes. A heated metal point is applied to one side of an animal's shoulder blade, or sometimes to the carapace of a tortoise [Plates 44–5]. This produces cracks on the other side, often running approximately at right angles to each other where they join. The interpretation of the shapes of these cracks decides the answers to the questions put to the oracle, and they are usually questions demanding a simple answer, yes or no. The use of oracle-bones is a feature, and a continuing feature, of the Shang civilization; and during the Shang period the whole technique of scapulimancy was improved. At Anyang itself, the spot where the hot metal was made to touch the bone was usually prepared by cutting a circular pit overlapped by an oval one. As has been said, 'The run of the cracks, and presumably the answers they gave, were thus to some extent predetermined.'[92]

It was natural that Chinese archaeologists and historians should want to know whence came these oracle-bones. Did they come from a Shang site? Could the Shang semi-historical dynasty be given an archaeological connotation? The search for the oracle-bones used by the Chinese apothecaries led to Hsiao T'un near Anyang, and the excavation of Hsiao T'un was started in 1928 by Tung Tso-pin. The work was then taken over by Le Chi as first field director from 1928 to 1937 of a large campaign organized by the National Research Institute of History and Philology of Academica Sinica, together with the Freer Gallery of Art of the Smithsonian Institution. Then came the war, and after the war the work was resumed. The Archaeological Institute of the Chinese Academy of Sciences was founded in 1949. Dr Hsai Nai resumed work at Anyang in 1950 and by 1959 it was possible to report that a total of 125 Shang sites had been excavated. The most important sites, like Anyang itself, are centred around modern cities. There in brief is the story of the discovery of the first Chinese civilization: it is a very recent affair. As Dr Chêng Tê-K'un says in the opening sentence of his second volume on *The Archaeology of China*: 'The archaeology of Shang China has a history of only thirty years.'

It is not the intention of this book to describe the first civilizations in the Old and New Worlds; our concern is with the origins of these civilizations as seen from a study of the archaeological material; but we must say a few words about the inhabitants of Anyang and the other Shang cities, concerning which the average reader may know even less than he does about the Sumerians or the ancient Egyptians or the dwellers in the Indus cities. The Shang people were farmers and at their time the north China plain teemed with busy life, and there was a large and growing population in villages and towns. They cultivated barley, wheat, millet (two kinds – yellow and black) and sorghum. They had pigs, dogs, sheep and oxen. Their cities were on the banks of rivers and, without doubt, much of their transport was by water – on rafts made of wood or bamboo. The crafts of the specialists and artists in the Shang cities included the carving of stone [Plate 55], jade (including the making of jade scoops for cleaning out the ears), ivory, bone and shell, the making of pottery, inlaid work of wood, bone, lacquer, the making of gold ornaments, the casting of copper, lead and bronze [Plate 56]. And much of this was brilliantly done. Chêng Tê-K'un says of the Shang craftsman: 'His ability, especially in the later periods, surpassed the mere confines of technical skill.' All this high craftsmanship was concentrated, of course, in the towns. There is very little indication of external trade although there must have been a certain amount since some of the materials used came from outside the borders of China.

The Shang civilization was a metal-using society. The Shang bronzes were eating and drinking vessels, cooking utensils and containers, tools and weapons, chariot- and horse-fittings and other ornaments [Plates 64–54]. Perhaps the most distinctive vessels were those used for sacrifices to the gods and to ancestors. Shang bronze craftsmanship has been described as 'one of the outstanding arts of the ancient world, narrow in range of expression, but astonishingly powerful'.

Many Shang bronzes are inscribed. These inscriptions are to be found in any part of the vessel – at the rim, on the shoulder, on the body, at the bottom, on the inside, on the cover, under the handle, and often incorporated in the decorative pattern. They are short, and either record an event (a war, rewards, etc.), or the name of a clan, an ancestor, the maker of the vessel, or the type-name of the vessel itself. The study of Shang writing is a very special branch of Chinese archaeology and epigraphy. Most of it is on the shells and bones used for oracle divination, and is known as *chia-ku-hsueh*, or the study of shell and bone writing.

The estimated number of inscribed shells and bones from Shang times found so far is in the neighbourhood of a hundred thousand; and there are three hundred Chinese scholars engaged in their decipherment and translation. These oracle records show that the Shang kings resorted to scapulimancy in all sorts of matters such as sacrificial ceremonies, natural phenomena (weather and harvests), crops and general agricultural queries, wars and military expeditions, and the private affairs of the king (such as trips, travel, sickness, dreams, childbirth, etc.), and general future well-being. Unfortunately, because the oracle inscriptions are mainly inquiries and answers by and to the Shang kings, they do not give us a full and clear picture of the Shang civilization. Their value is further restricted by the fact that some of the Shang kings were not devoted to scapulimancy. Those who were are exemplified by King Wu-ting: he consulted the oracle on practically everything concerning his life, and when he had a toothache he even resorted to divination to find out which of his ancestors was responsible for it.

The Shang oracle script stemmed directly from an earlier form which was pictographic. Tung Tso-pin argued that the earliest Chinese writing developed independently among the Neolithic peasant villagers of the third millennium B.C. The rise of the Shang royal house, and the development of a political city centre improved and developed the writing. It was the necessity for labelling private property as well as the keeping of historical records, and the records of the oracles, that made all this happen.

Cowrie shells were a medium of trade and exchange. King Wu-ting, whom we have already mentioned, gave his daughters two strings of cowrie shells each: they were strung five on a string, and a pair of them constituted a *p'eng* – ten digits made up the Shang unit of counting – the decimal system. The Shang people calculated time in units of ten and a hundred days.

Shang society was organized into two strata – the ruling warrior nobility and the village farmers: it was, in the words of Chêng Tê-K'un, 'a bifurcated society which has remained the chief characteristic of Chinese society ever since'. The Shang people worshipped their ancestors and many heavenly gods and earthly deities. They had a wide variety of rituals conducted by priests and shamans and accompanied by music and dances. There is no way to reconstruct the music itself, but a large number of musical instruments have been found including drums, ocarinas, the *ching* chiming stones of jade and marble, and bells.

The founding of the Shang capital at Anyang by King P'an Keng, who moved there from further east, is dated to 1384 B.C., and the end of the Shang dynasty to 1122 B.C. But we know now that Anyang was a late Shang capital. The present accepted chronology is shown below.

Proto-Shang, still a Neolithic phase	2500 to 2100 B.C.
Early Shang	2100 to 1750 B.C.
Middle Shang, the 'early dynastic period'	1750 to 1400 B.C.
Late Shang	1400 to 1100 B.C.

Our main concern here is how the Shang civilization came into existence. The transition from the Neolithic peasant-villagers to the Bronze Age city-dwellers seems mysterious, sudden and abrupt. In the course of a few centuries the villagers fell under the domination of walled cities whose rulers had bronze weapons, chariots and slaves. What happened? Did the Shang culture come from the west? or did it develop in eastern Asia – in China itself? Was there a local synoecism? Are we observing in China a test case in our experimental study of the origins of civilization? Was there, if we may use this phrase, a sino-synoecism as there was a Sumerian synoecism, and an Egyptian synoecism, and an Indus Valley synoecism? We have distinguished two processes amidst the synoecisms of western Asia and Egypt: we have argued that the Sumerian synoecism was original and unattended by outside influences – and how could it have been otherwise? After all, there were no earlier civilizations. But we have suggested that the process in Egypt and the Indus Valley was different: in those areas a developing synoecism was stimulated by idea-diffusion from Mesopotamia.

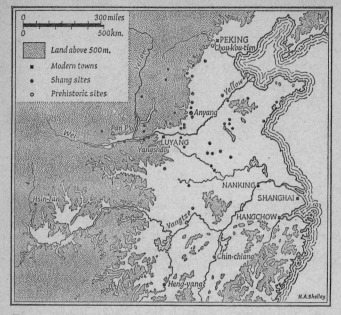

Figure 11. Area of the Shang civilization, showing principal sites

The Sumerians were responsible in part, if perhaps in very small part, for the eventual emergence of the Egyptian and Indus civilizations. But what about Shang China? Is it an outpost of the Sumerians, if not by actual migration, by some process of idea- or stimulus-diffusion? Was it, like the Indus civilization, a native development which was spurred on and excited by contacts with the more ancient west? Or is the answer that Shang China represents an entirely independent process of synoecism?

Let us make no mistake about one thing: after forty years of archaeological research in China it is clear that

Shang civilization is much later than the civilizations of Sumer and Egypt, and perhaps later than, or at least contemporary with, the Indus civilization. There is, therefore, no chronological reason why Shang China should not be a colony of the west. We have already spoken of the east-west route, and if this route worked for the Greeks and for Marco Polo, and could have worked in the time of the Neolithic peasant farmers, there is clearly no reason why it could not have existed in the third millennium B.C.

There can be no question that Shang society is in many ways very like the city-states of the Bronze Age Near East. Watson puts the comparison very well when he says:

A king due to be deified after death, ruler in a kind of theocracy; holocausts of human victims at royal funerals, pillared palaces, walls built of stamped earth, carving of hard stone (jade) and rudimentary sculpture, an armament based on the chariot and the bow, some form of slavery (possibly recruited freely from prisoners of war) and a system of writing which combines ideographic and phonetic principles.

But is parallelism due to parallel development or to diffusion? One of the key issues is the working of bronze, and the knowledge of bronze metallurgy is really the nub of the problem. In South-West Asia and Europe there was a primitive stage of bronze metallurgy with open moulds used for casting simple flat axes, daggers and pins. In China this does not happen: the bronzesmiths start, straight away, with a complicated metallurgy. From the very beginning they are making elaborate ornamental ritual vessels [Plates 46–9]. Li Chi has studied the Shang bronzes in detail and shows that most of them can be traced back to non-metal prototypes.

There are various solutions to this problem of the origins of bronze metallurgy in China. The first is a full-scale invasion of people from the west, who settled down as predatory aristocrats among and over the Neolithic autochthones. The second is 'technological influence', and this is Watson's view. 'The knowledge of bronze-casting,' he says, 'must have travelled eastwards from the Near East as the germ of a technological and social revolution. . . . It seems undeniable that the knowledge of bronze-casting came to China from the west.' But this is not the view held by Chinese archaeologists writing in the last few years. Chêng Tê-K'un believes that bronze-working was independently invented in China: it was not, he says, 'a gift from heaven, nor was it introduced by invaders from Western Asia'.[93]

But there are western forms in China, such as a particular form of spearhead, the socketed axe, animal-headed knives like those of south Siberia, and perhaps some chariot parts – and indeed possibly the very idea of a chariot and its design. What is certain is that, even if the idea of bronze technology came from the west, that technique was soon completely naturalized in China. The Shang bronze industry is Chinese in style and flavour from the very beginning. Watson puts this well when he says, while insisting on the fact that the technique of casting must have come from the west, 'in the forms which the bronze was used to produce, and in art, the culture of the Chinese city states as a whole is an individual growth'.

It would now seem to most people that the Shang cities themselves are the result of individual growth. Here, as in southern Mesopotamia, we are observing an independent process of synoecism, and the development of Chinese archaeology is gradually and continually working out the succession of prehistoric cultures from the earliest Yang Shao Neolithic to the full Shang cities. Chinese civilization was, then, born in the Yellow River and by local growth there: it does not seem to have had the stimulus-diffusion from

Sumer for which we argued in Egypt and the Indus Valley; but it does seem to have borrowed some cultural features from the west – and this small list of borrowings probably or almost certainly included the technique of bronze-working.

CHAPTER SIX

THE DISCOVERY OF THE
AMERICAN CIVILIZATIONS

In 1493 'a certayne caravelle' captained 'by the very magnificent lord Don Cristobal Colon ... sayling the West Ocean ... was driven to a land unknowne, and not described by any Map or Carde of the Sea'. Admiral Christopher Columbus, looking for the Indies, had discovered America. In the last few years the discovery of America by the world of western and Mediterranean Europe has become once again a matter of public curiosity and heated interest. The publication of the Vinland map has made people ask again how far the Vikings got into America, and whether Columbus and the Mediterranean sea-captains of the fifteenth century knew of the Vikings or of previous voyages to the Americas – if there were any. All the old hares have been started up, all the follies brought out. Madoc's possible journeys to America from Wales in the twelfth century A.D. are being re-canvassed, and an Italian Professor in a public lecture in Florence declared that the Etruscans had got to what is now Guyana in the twelfth century B.C.[94]

We must distinguish very clearly here between the facts, if any, of the discovery of America by the late medieval and modern world before 1492, and the possibility or improbability of Europeans getting to America before Columbus. Whether there were Vikings, Welshmen or Etruscans in America before Columbus (and there certainly were Vikings but most likely no Welshmen or Etruscans), for the modern world, the world we are concerned with which began to be interested in its remote prehistoric and less remote proto-historic origins, America begins with Columbus.

But he did not discover what are now generally referred to as the pre-Columbian civilizations. In the Caribbean he found not civilized people but savages, and in his *Journal* he describes them as having handsome bodies and good faces, noting that they wore their hair over their eyebrows, that some were painted black, some white and some red, and that some had 'spears tipped with fishes teeth'. They brought him presents of parrots, and to his shipmates balls of cotton thread. They came out to his ship in boats made of hollowed tree-trunks, richly carved, and propelled by paddles not unlike peels or bakers' shovels.

Columbus's men established the first permanent settlement in Hispaniola in 1493. Shortage of native labour and the hope of finding gold drove the Spanish on. In 1513 Balboa's explorations showed that there was only a narrow strip of land between the two great oceans – the Atlantic and the Pacific. Everywhere there was gossip of rich and powerful cities, unknown civilizations, mystery beyond the mountains. In 1519 an expedition from Cuba led by Cortés landed at Vera Cruz and made its way through the mountains to the great capital city of Tenochtitlán, which eventually fell in 1521. Cortés kidnapped Moctezuma, the head war-chief, and brought to an abrupt end a civilization, that of the Aztecs, whose existence he was the first European to discover.

One of Cortés's most able lieutenants, Pedro de Alvarado, went on to conquer the highland area of Guatemala, founding a Spanish city there in 1524. The chief cities of Yucatán were all subdued with great brutality by the Spaniards, the 'men of Mexico' as they were called. After five years of coastal exploration south from Panama, Francisco Pizarro, with only 180 men, landed on the north coast of Peru in 1530.

Three years later, he and his army, now 600 men, took and sacked the city of Cuzco, the capital of the Incas. Pizarro brought the Inca Empire to an end in one single November afternoon in 1533.[95]

Thus, in fifteen years, between 1519 and 1533, the western world, the world of Western and Mediterranean Europe, which then thought, and not unnaturally, that it *was* civilization and that there were no other civilizations, discovered and conquered – the right phrase might be brutally destroyed – three civilizations, that of the Aztecs of Mexico, the Maya of Yucatán and Guatemala, and the Incas of Peru.

Here in America we are dealing with an historical and archaeological phenomenon which is quite different from that of the discovery of ancient Sumer, ancient Egypt, the ancient cities of the Indus Valley, or the archaeological discovery of the Shang civilization of China. These were discovered by the spade, for the decipherment of the Rosetta Stone and the Behistun inscription only got one or two stages further back than known ancient history. It was the spade at Naqada and Merimba, at Ur and Erech, at Anyang and Harappa that has got us really further back. But the old civilizations – the old proto-historic and prehistoric civilizations – of Central and Southern America were alive and kicking, though admittedly not sufficiently alive, or kicking efficiently enough to dispose of the Spaniards, in the early sixteenth century A.D. The conquistadors had, in a few years, gone back three to four millennia, and in America in the sixteenth century, Europe met, if not its own past, at least a form of its own past – and alive.

A few words about the ancient civilizations which the Europeans met in America. The Aztecs who founded the city of Tenochtitlán, which afterwards became Mexico City, were an extremely warlike people: they worked gold and copper, had a system of counting based on twenty, a calendar and hieroglyphic writing. At its zenith, Tenochtitlán was a city of some three hundred thousand inhabitants. It was divided into what we might call wards or *arrondissements*, each inhabited by a group of related craftsmen and their families. The site of Mexico City is near a great obsidian quarry and the Aztec obsidian-knappers made blades for razors and swords and other tools, which were exported extensively. The Aztec craftsmen also worked in jade and were skilled goldsmiths, casting the gold in simple moulds and also in *cire-perdue* moulds. They were superb jewellers, but only a small portion of their jewellery has survived: it was loot for the Spanish and was melted down by them. Occasionally an unlooted tomb is found such as that dug by Afonso Caso at Monte Albán in 1923.

Metal-working may have been as much as three hundred years old in Mexico at the time of the Spanish conquest. The Aztec metalsmiths melted and cast copper – mainly in the form of bells. Copper intended for tools like knives was beaten cold. At the time of the conquest copper had not yet begun to replace obsidian and polished stone: the Aztecs were, to use the technological terms of the Old World model of prehistory, in the Chalcolithic stage. The Aztecs had pyramids, but they were not tombs like the Egyptian pyramids. More like the Sumerian *ziggurats* [Plates 1, 2] they were – as a happy phrase has it – theatres in reverse. At the summit of the pyramid [Plates 64–5, 77–8] was an altar and idols to the gods, and from this high position the priests conducted human sacrifices: they opened up the chosen victims with obsidian knives and held up the still quivering hearts to the great crowds around. These Aztec pyramids were of stone but made by stone tools – there was little or no use of metal tools in their construction.

The Aztecs and the Maya, as well as some other groups in Mexico, made books of deerskin on which they wrote with paint. The writing was pictographic like Egyptian hieroglyphs. Moctezuma had a house full of these deerskin books: they were not literature – they were the accounts of his kitchens. We are reminded of the nature of the first Sumerian records, also lists and inventories.

The Aztec system of counting in twenties – the vigesimal system – was very different from the Old World systems that worked in tens and dozens. Their calculations involved zero and the place system, both unknown in western Europe until brought by the Arabs from India.

The Spanish conquerors discovered the Maya in Guatemala, Honduras, and the south of Mexico, living in tropical forests and mountains. There is little doubt in most peoples' minds that the Maya produced the highest civilization that was developed in America in pre-conquest times. The history of the Maya is divided into two principal periods – the Old Empire, which flourished for above five hundred years between the second and the seventh century A.D., and the New Empire, which was established about A.D. 1000 and lasted until the arrival of the Spaniards in the sixteenth century.

The Maya were fine builders and had fine sculptors. A typical Maya city had a spacious religious and civic centre with courts and pyramidal platforms. The Old Maya Empire collapsed for reasons not known soon after A.D. 600. Then the people left their cities and gradually migrated northwards finally settling about A.D. 1000 in part of the south Mexican state of Yucatán. The New Empire built large courts for their semi-religious ball-game, the finest of which is still to be seen in the town of Chichen Itzá in Yucatán. For this ball-game, a simplified version of which is still played

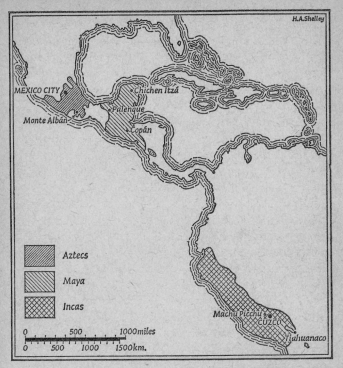

Figure 12. Areas of the Inca, Maya and Aztec civilizations

today in parts of Mexico, a large solid rubber ball was used, and one of the chief objects of the game was to knock the ball through stone rings fixed high up on the sides of the court.

The Maya of the jungles of Yucatán, Guatemala and Honduras had no metal at all except a very few gold and copper ornaments. It was with stone tools, and stone tools alone, that they made their elaborate temples and pyramids and their tall stelae which are covered with bas-reliefs and hieroglyphs. Neither the Maya nor the Aztec civilization had animals capable of bearing burdens. Aztec trade was effected by using the backs of human beings for conveying goods, but the Aztecs had boats and did short journeys by paddling and punting their boats along.

The basis of Mayan life, as of life in the other Central American civilizations, was an agriculture based on three crops: maize, beans and squash. These were garden plants; cultivation was by the hoe, and it all was, in a way, horticulture rather than agriculture.[96]

When the Spaniards conquered Peru in 1533 they found a vast empire, the empire of the Incas, extending from Ecuador in the north to about the middle of Chile in the south, a distance of more than 2,000 miles and including a considerable part of the highlands of Bolivia and the Argentine, but on the east stopping short of the tropical forests of the Amazon basin. The Incas were so called from their king, the Inca: and the great Inca was thought to be the offspring of the sun. Theirs was a highland civilization and their capital was Cuzco, which is 11,000 feet above sea-level. Their empire followed very roughly the lines of the Andes mountains but included the narrow strip of lowland on the Pacific coast.

The Inca state was very highly organized, and was dominated by the supreme ruler, the Inca, and by his royal clan. The Incas had no form of writing and no form of money, but they kept accurate accounts by means of elaborately knotted and coloured strings called *quipus*. They had a vast system of terrace agriculture, and built great fortresses with walls which are practically indestructible. Along the whole extent of the plateau and the coast the Incas had built a network of roads as good as those of the Romans in Europe. In the mountains these are narrow and built of stone; the great coastal road was 30 feet wide and banked with high clay walls to keep out the sand. Over deep chasms the Inca engineers had suspension bridges of rope. Along these roads the officials of the Inca Empire travelled on foot to keep order in the land, collect taxes, and to see to the organization of trade. There was an imperial messenger system and with this system and the good roads, the Incas were able successfully to govern a number of peoples speaking different languages.

The Incas were, technologically speaking, in a full Bronze Age when discovered by the Spaniards. Their craftsmen made knives, chisels and axes of a mixture of copper and tin, but these tools were not hard enough to cut the rock used in many of their buildings. Their great buildings, like those of the Maya and the Aztecs, were fashioned with stone tools.

The Incas were well informed about matters astronomical and had calculated the length of the solar year by means of what can only be called observatories. They had made many remarkable advances in surgery and were able to perform successfully very difficult operations. In the coastal cities the Incas worked at rows of looms: there seems little doubt that the ancient people of Peru mass-produced textiles. The wool and cotton goods found in several hundreds of Inca graves are thought by many competent judges to be among the finest ever woven anywhere in the world.

The quality of the Inca civilization is beyond any dispute. In the highlands they had learnt to cultivate the potato and the quinoa. They had also domesticated two small members of the camel family, namely the llama and the alpaca. These provided beasts of burden for transport as well as wool, manure and meat.[97]

When Cortés and Pizarro penetrated Mexico and Peru

they were exploring a new world, the new world of the Americas, but they also entered the past, and found the old world of the Americas. As Carleton Coon has said, what these conquistadors of the early sixteenth century succeeded in doing was what every archaeologist dreams of doing, namely, stepping backwards in time:

When Cortés and his men entered the valley of Mexico, they marched into an Early Metal Age civilization comparable in many respects with that of Egypt in late pre-dynastic and early dynastic times, and that of early Sumer. It was as if, when Sir Leonard Woolley had uncovered the ramp to a royal tomb at Ur, the kings and queens and soldiers and maidens had all come to life and offered him a cup of tea.[98]

The Aztecs, the Maya and the Incas were not what the Spaniards were expecting. They were expecting India. But what they discovered was a lost world – a lost civilized world. The discovery of these lost civilizations posed a remarkable question to the thinking people of the sixteenth century and later in Europe – the question of the origins of man's culture and more especially that high culture that turned into civilization. As we see it today, there was a triple question: First, how did savage man get to America? Secondly, how did the barbarian societies of America, that is to say, the first agricultural or horticultural societies, come into existence? And, in the third place, how did the civilized American societies happen?[99]

The third question is our main concern here: How did the civilizations of Central America and Peru come into existence? What is the origin of the civilizations of Mesoamerica, and of Nuclear America in general? Let us get the use of these terms clear in our minds. Mesoamerica was defined by Paul Kirchoff as comprising the Mexican and Mayan civilizations. By Nuclear America is meant the southern two-thirds of Mexico, all Central America, Andean and coastal Colombia, Ecuador and Peru with the adjacent parts of Bolivia. This was the heartland of native American agriculture and of the native pre-Columbian civilizations.

The American prehistoric and proto-historic civilizations have until recently received scant attention in the main schools of archaeology in Europe. This was not only because of lack of interest: it was for long thought by many that pre-Columbian America was unimportant; that the really important things in the history of early man and his civilization were the Neolithic and Urban Revolutions in the Near East. Gordon Childe, consciously and unconsciously, did much to foster this attitude. In his *What Happened in History* – a provocative title anyhow, as what he had to say stopped fifteen hundred years ago – first published in 1942, he stressed that what he was studying was 'the main stream' of history. This book is still in print and so it should be; it is a good, persuasive account of the origins of civilization in the ancient Near East. At the same time it is circumscribed – it has no account of Shang China and nothing about the ancient civilizations of America: you will look in vain in the index for Anyang, Aztecs, Incas, Maya, Peru. Childe was the most distinguished representative of the late nineteenth-century and early twentieth-century school of prehistorians and proto-historians who saw the problem of the past as the problem of the origins of European civilization – the problem of what lay behind Greece and Rome. And this was the most ancient Near East – Sumer, the Fertile Crescent, Egypt. I once tackled Childe about his neglect of the civilizations of Nuclear America, and he dismissed my question with the words, 'Never been there – peripheral and highly suspect.' In a recently published book entitled *Primitive Societies*, Professor Stuart Piggott writes: 'We cannot escape the feeling that Mesoamerican culture, even at its highest, is no more than (to adopt a phrase of the seventeenth-century writer Roger North), "such as an extraordinary high-spirited judicious Barbarian might be supposed originally to invent".' As I said in reviewing this book in the *Spectator*, surely 'all the seven early civilizations of man were invented by barbarians'. Apart from the barbarian agriculturists there was no one else to invent civilization, and that they did so is a tribute to their judgement and high spirits. The civilizations of China and Nuclear America are not in the main stream of the development of western European civilization; but they are civilizations, and the archaeological evidence for their genesis is of great value in studying the archaeological evidence for the genesis of the ancient civilizations of Nile, Tigris-Euphrates and Indus.

We cannot dismiss the third question we have asked ourselves, the question of the origin of the American pre-Columbian civilizations, by saying that they were not civilizations or that they were only half-way to civilization. By the definition we have adopted here, the Aztecs and the Maya and the Incas were civilized; their societies can be compared, if on a lower level of achievement – and we need not be dogmatic about this – with those of the ancient Egyptians and the Sumerians, the people of Mohenjo-daro and Harappa and the people of Shang China. Indeed one person thought them more civilized than was the western world: that person was Albrecht Dürer. In 1520 Dürer saw in Antwerp the treasure which the Aztec chief Moctezuma gave – if 'gave' is the right word – to Cortes for Charles V, and which Charles V sent round to be shown in various vassal towns. Antwerp was one of these towns, and there Dürer wrote, '*Et j'ai rien vu en ma vie qui eut réjoui mon coeur tant comme ces choses.*'

For the most part the old civilizations of the New World were forgotten again after their discovery. The Spanish and Portuguese were not really curious about them, and the people of North America, as Jacquetta Hawkes has said, 'had not the time. Most of them were too busy building a new civilization to give much thought to old ones.'[100] But later the Old World began to interest itself in the antiquity of the New World; in the late eighteenth century Louis XVI sent the French doctor and naturalist Eugène Dombey to Peru to describe and excavate, and Dombey's collections are to be found in Madrid and in the Musée de l'Homme in Paris. The first serious survey of Central American monuments was made under the auspices of Charles IV of Spain who sent a Frenchman, Captain Guillaume Dupaix, together with a Spanish draughtsman Castenada to report on Mexican ruins, and they made three expeditions between 1805 and 1807. The process was beginning: the archaeological traveller was discovering, in the late eighteenth and the nineteenth century, what direct contact had seen and destroyed only three hundred years before.

Then, secure in their own newly created civilization, the people of post-Columbian America began to study pre-Columbian times; in the last half century they have poured money and initiative and energy into the study of the past of the New World. By now they have produced, through a brilliant series of planned reconnaissances and excavations, the answers to the three questions about the past of the native Americans, answers which throw much light not only on the past of America, but are of fundamental import to any general study of the origins of civilization in the world as a whole.

We in Europe adopted a technological model to help us deal with the archaeological material in the early and middle nineteenth century; it was a good one, and a useful one, though now of very limited use. This is why the textbooks speak of Palaeolithic, Neolithic, Bronze Age and Iron Age – the Four Ages of Lubbock, developed from the Three Ages of Thomsen. At first American archaeologists used this kind of terminology for the descriptive analysis of the pre-Columbian materials they were studying, but it was not a happy system and soon they began to produce new systems and a new terminology, which we will discuss in the next chapter. Let us now turn to the various views that have been put forward for the origins of the Americans and American civilization, often without a shred of archaeological evidence.[101]

Many of the theories put forward, often with passion and fervour – sometimes a religious passion and a mystical fervour – had no regard for facts or the way that facts can be marshalled and manipulated in a scholarly, humane and scientific framework of argument. The problem of the origins of man and civilization in America provides one of the classic examples of how a problem of real scholarship can bring out all the crackpots. Harry Gladwin may be right in dubbing all of us who appear to him to toe the establishment line in these matters as 'Phuddy-Duddies' – his very nice name for people who have taken their Ph.D. – if he means by that name the entrenched scholars. We are certainly right in calling the many men and women we shall soon be discussing the crackpots of the lunatic fringe of archaeology, anthropology and ancient history. Every conceivable theory has been put forward about the origin of man and his civilization, in America as elsewhere, and this is why we are discussing here the light which archaeology throws on this problem. For it cuts a swathe through the wild grasses that grow on the lunatic fringes of those difficult meadows where, suitably cultivated, truth begins to be discernible. The professional study of American archaeology is not necessarily infallible, and it is still young, compared with the archaeology of Europe and the Near East; but the results it has already achieved in a relatively short period are little short of sensational. These results we shall discuss in the next chapter; here and now our concern is with the non-archaeological theories of American origins, or, to put it better, the theories of American origins which relied on non-existent or misrepresented facts.

These theories have been summarized in a delightful book published in 1962 by the University of Chicago Press: it is entitled *Lost Tribes and Sunken Continents* and was written by Robert Wauchope, Professor of Anthropology at Tulane University and Director of the Middle American Research Institute. It could be argued that this book, and what I am about to say, is just a calendar of human frailties and follies that was best forgotten, or remembered only by the historians of archaeology and anthropology, and of the tendency in mankind to seek for the comforts of unreason. But this is not so: the very same theories are continually cropping up, and the reader of this book will be leading an unusually fortunate and sheltered life if he does not at some time meet some of these Lunatic Fringers.

As I have already said, the publication of the Vinland map has started up again all the old hares and, if we may mix the metaphor, all the old hobby-horses are being ridden hard again. Let us first be clear about the relevance of the Vinland map – which some argue Columbus may have seen – to this general problem. A large land mass called Antillia appears on almost all maps of the fifteenth and early sixteenth centuries. Columbus consulted Toscanelli's chart in 1474; it shows Antillia directly on the track from the Canary Islands to Japan. Columbus is said to have shaped his course to this island, and to have sailed due west for sixteen hundred miles looking for it. Whether the existence of Antillia on this and other maps is a memory of the Vikings and their discovery of America, or is a pure invention, is neither here nor there.

What is very much to the point is that the Vikings themselves certainly got to America. How far down the coast of eastern America they got to we do not know. It used to be said that Vinland must mean the land of vines and that the Vikings must therefore have got to a latitude far enough south to meet wild grapes. But on the other hand we are told that Vinland does not mean Wineland but just meadowland.[102]

There is certainly very little archaeological evidence for the Vikings south of their known Greenland settlements. Archaeological evidence has from time to time been alleged to exist, and nowhere more vociferously, and with some show of authority, than in the claims made for the Kensington Stone from Minnesota. This has been repeatedly claimed as a great American antiquity, but it seems to be a late nineteenth-century forgery. Recently, however, an interesting site, possibly of the Vikings, has been found in Newfoundland at a place called L'Anse aux Meadows. It has been excavated by Helge Ingstad of Oslo who has found archaeological material suggesting a tenth-century date, and this confirmed by C14 dating.

But this tenth-century date proves no more than that the Vikings may have brought European civilization to America; for man was in existence in that continent long before the Vikings, and – what is more important – had created civilizations there centuries before their time.

The same difficulty applies to St Brendan and to Madoc:

these Irish and Welsh Christian travellers could not have taken civilization from the Celtic west to America because there were civilized societies there long before them. And the same is true of the bizarre and very strange idea of Harold S. Gladwin, whose *Men Out of Asia*, published in 1947, suggested, among many other strange ideas, that the survivors of the wrecked fleet of Alexander the Great found their way to America in the fourth century B.C., and created some of the early American civilizations.

The Lost Tribes of Israel hypothesis is open to the same objections. Viscount Kingsborough propounded this doctrine in his nine-volume work entitled *The Antiquities of Mexico*, published between 1831 and 1848. Kingsborough was convinced that the Mexicans were descendants of the ten (or, as some say, the nine and a half) tribes of Israel that were carried away by the King of Assyria from Samaria in 422 B.C. Of course, Kingsborough was not the first person to set out this theory. It had been canvassed from 1533 onwards, but it was Kingsborough who set it out at the greatest length, and, for that matter, *ad nauseam*.

It is widely held by many people that *The Book of Mormon* is concerned with the doctrine of the Lost Tribes of Israel and their migration to America, but this is not true. It is, however, true that the Church of Jesus Christ of Latter-day Saints has been active in proving – or one might more wisely say trying to prove – that Jews came from the Mediterranean to America and there founded the first pre-Columbian civilization. Article 8, Chapter 15 of the *Articles of Faith for the Book of Mormon* sets out the beliefs of the Church that America was settled by Jaredites who came directly from the tower of Babel, and who were succeeded by Israelites from Jerusalem who built the great pre-Columbian cities of Nuclear America. The Jaredites, in this exposition, were Sumerians. To the Mediterranean and Near Eastern ancestors of the Middle American civilizations we must add the Phoenicians, the Carthaginians and the Etruscans; there is scarcely a people that superficial and indisciplined students of the problem of American origins have not put forward.

But of all the people acclaimed as the progenitors of the ancient American civilizations the most popular have been the ancient Egyptians, and the person principally responsible for this was Sir Grafton Elliot Smith. Elliot Smith was an Australian who became Professor of Anatomy successively in Cairo, Manchester, and London. He was a great anatomist, a brilliant teacher and an excellent scholar in his work on human palaeontology. But he had a kink: when he studied mummies in Egypt and found the technique of mummification very highly complicated – although, in fact, it is the standard procedure for dealing with any dead animals – he believed it was a technique that could not have been independently invented elsewhere. This naturally drove Elliot Smith to study mummification in other parts of the world, and there, or so he thought, he found the same techniques and ritual as existed in ancient Egypt. It all must therefore have started in Egypt: so he and his disciple, W. J. Perry, had Egyptians spreading a Heliolithic Civilization all over the world. By the way, Ancient Egypt in America is still a popular cult although of course there is no basis for it whatsoever.

But let us not linger with the more obvious 'lost tribes' any longer; there are many more tribes and nations that could be listed in this sad catalogue – Trojans, Romans, Greeks, Scythians, Tartars, Chinese, Indians, Mandingoes and many other African tribes, Madagascans, Basques, Portuguese, Huns – at some time or other almost every known people has been pressed into the origins-of-America service. But the best theories are those that bring the origins of American civilization from lost continents, either the continent of Atlantis or the continent of Lemuria or Mu. And here their protagonists are unassailable: the continents have gone, their imagined great civilizations have disappeared, and we cannot with certainty prove that they did not exist.

This is, indeed, a calendar of lunacies, and as we look through the list of suggested American origins, we know that the crackpots are with us. But what do the present professional archaeologists and anthropologists say? What is the view today of those men amusingly labelled Phuddy-Duddies? They say four things important to our present inquiry. The first is that outlined by Thomas Jefferson in his *Note on the State of Virginia*: namely, that America was first peopled by invaders coming from Asia across the Bering Straits to Alaska between 50,000 and 25,000 years ago. Secondly, it is now said that agriculture (or horticulture, if you prefer this term) was independently invented in America, and perhaps independently invented in three or four areas. In the third place they say that some of these indigenous American agricultural economies developed into urban civilizations without outside intervention; that is to say, there was a native process of synoecism, and to the Chinese synoecism we must now add the Mesoamerican or Nuclear-American synoecism. The fourth point we have listed, and to which we will come back in the next chapter, is this: Was there some outside influence, or were there some outside influences, that were felt during the process or the processes of American synoecism? And I quote here, so that the reader should not think I am entirely prejudiced in this matter, the statement of Robert Wauchope when he says: 'A growing number of anthropologists also think that certain American high civilizations, like the Maya, received some additional stimulus from trans-Pacific contacts with south-east Asia.'

The four essential items in this brief and bald statement will be discussed in some detail in the next chapter, but we must not end this chapter without observing how the tables were turned by one or two of those nimble-witted but light-headed pseudo-scholars who write about these matters. A few of them have taken up the position that man originated in America and spread himself and his civilization from Nuclear America to the Western World – to the Mediterranean and Egypt. This is the reverse of Egypt in America: this is America in Egypt and Sumer. Perhaps the best comment on all this nonsense of hypothetical origins without archaeological foundation is provided by some paragraphs in the *Way of the World* feature of the English *Daily Telegraph* for 2 November 1965. This feature, signed with the pseudonym 'Peter Simple', is full of amusing and satirical comment. Under the title 'Our Aztec Heritage', he writes:

An American historian, Dr Howard Sandstorm, has put forward a new theory that the Aztecs discovered Europe in the Seventh Century. He believes that several expeditions crossed the North Atlantic in stone boats, using the recently devised Aztec stone compass and other navigational aids. Landing on the west coast of Britain, they took advantage of the disturbed conditions of the time to push inland to what are now the Midlands, in search of terrain resembling that of their native Central America. Though disappointed in this, they established several colonies in the Stretchford area, Dr Sandstorm believes, before succumbing to the damp conditions and a general feeling of discouragement and of not being quite 'all there'.

His theory is supported by discoveries made by amateur archaeologists in the area during the last few years. These include a small stone fragment of a step-pyramid unearthed dur-ing excavations for the new M6, and a piece of obsidian thought to be part of a tear-off stone calendar, found in a trans-port café at Lampton-on-Hoke. A local scholar, the Reverend J. S. Instep of Nerdley, states in his book *Our Aztec Heritage*, that there is a recognizable Aztec strain in the Stretchford popu-lation even today, and that Aztec customs, such as large-scale human sacrifice, have never completely died out.

This satirical comment is the best answer that can be given to all the strange lunatic theorists about the origin of the peoples and the civilizations of pre-Columbian America; but, in their excuse, if not in their defence, it must be said that it is only in the last ten years that the true and chrono-logically well-attested picture of American origins has be-come available to scholars. One always hopes, and not, I think, in vain, that the lunatic fringes of archaeology will narrow, if not disappear, as precise archaeological informa-tion and precise dates provided by C14 dating reduce the area in which speculation is possible. As we shall see in the next chapter, it is no longer possible to speculate on the origins of the pre-Columbian Americans and their progress from savagery through barbarism to civilization. We now have the facts. Speculation must be confined to the process.

CHAPTER SEVEN

ARCHAEOLOGY AND THE DEVELOP-
MENT OF AMERICAN CIVILIZATION

In chapter six it was said that the consensus of opinion among archaeologists and anthropologists working on pre-Columbian America was that that continent was first peopled by folk coming across the Bering Straits to Alaska between 50,000 and 25,000 years ago, that agriculture was independently invented in America, that some of the early agricultural communities there developed into civilizations by an indigenous process of synoecism, and that a number of American anthropologists now believe that some of the native high cultures and civilizations may have received ideas and stimuli from outside, though no serious scholar believes in an invasion by any one of that long catalogue of people mentioned in the last chapter. This last matter, outside stimuli of a limited kind, is a controversial matter. Let us first concentrate on the three points on which there is general agreement – the first peopling of America, the independent American origin of agriculture, and the synoecism in Nuclear America.[103]

In the nineteenth century, archaeologists working on the prehistory of Europe devised a technological model: the model that is generally referred to as the Three-Age system of Thomsen and the Four-Age system of Lubbock. At first American archaeologists used the Four-Age system of Palaeolithic, Neolithic, Bronze Age and Iron Age, but they soon began to devise new systems and a new terminology. These are discussed by Willey and Phillips in their book

Methods and Aims in American Archaeology first published in 1958, where they set out the terminology now widely used in American archaeology of five periods, namely, Lithic, Archaic, Formative, Classic and post-Classic.

The Lithic and Archaic stages need not detain us long. They correspond in a very general way to the Upper Palaeolithic and Mesolithic of Europe and the Near East. The Lithic stage saw man in the western part of northern America somewhere between 30,000 and 20,000 years ago: some seven hundred generations and perhaps 18,000 years later man had reached the southern tip of south America. He was certainly there by 7000 B.C. It has been estimated that the journey of 11,000 miles from the Bering Straits to the Cape Horn area meant an average of 18.3 miles per generation. These early dates are not as yet accepted by all American archaeologists: what there is no disagreement about is that man, that is to say the earliest American Indian, was in what is now the United States of America by between 12,000 and 10,000 B.C.

The people of the Lithic stage were mainly hunters: those of the Archaic stage were migratory hunters and food gatherers living in environments which approximated to present-day conditions. Some of these Archaic-stage food gatherers moved slowly to food production. A generation and more of detailed archaeological research in Mesoamerica has shown that there was no Neolithic or food-producing 'revolution' here, but a slow process of experimentation and development. The change from the Archaic stage of food gathering to effective village farming occupied the period from 6500 to 1000 B.C. There was a long period of incipient agriculture based on a few domestic plants, mainly maize.

Maize was unknown in the Old World until after Columbus, whereas it was the basic plant of *all* the pre-Columbian

Figure 13. Areas of independent agricultural invention in America

advanced cultures and civilizations. It seemed certain, then, that maize had been domesticated in America, even though no living wild form of corn had hitherto been found in the Americas. Then, since 1961, in the valley of Tehuacán, a dry valley in southern Mexico, five caves have been excavated in which the food remains of early peoples were preserved to a remarkable degree, and in stratified deposits. Professor MacNeish, who conducted these most important excavations, believes he has shown that the wild ancestor of maize was domesticated in this area about the beginning of the fifth millennium B.C. The earliest remains, which he dates to between 5200 and 3400 B.C., contain certainly wild corn. Later remains include cultivated corn and reveal an evolutionary sequence that gave rise to the several still-existing Mexican races of maize.

This archaeological-cum-botanical field research which actually produced the wild precursor of maize, a wild plant which has died out, is one of the most exciting of recent archaeological discoveries. Professor MacNeish, in a recent survey, describes four areas in Nuclear America where agriculture came into being. The first we have just referred to: south Central Mexico. The second was in southern Tamaulipas in north-eastern Mexico near the Gulf Coast; here the domesticates were gourds, pumpkins, runner beans, chili and later, corn. A third area was the arid coastal region of northern Peru: incipient agriculture began here with gourds and lima beans; subsequently, cotton, chili, and two kinds of squash were grown, and in the final stage of incipient agriculture in Peru (1200 to 750 B.C.) there was maize. In the Peruvian Formative period from 750 B.C. to the beginning of the Christian are, the Peruvian villages, based on full-time agriculture supplemented by irrigation, included in their list of crops not only those already

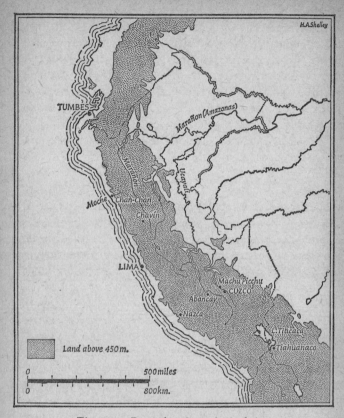

Figure 14. Peru, showing principal sites

mentioned but common beans, manioc, peanuts, potatoes, sweet potatoes and avocados. The fourth area was in the south-west of the U.S.A. Here a site in central New Mexico yielded, from perhaps as early as 4000 B.C., gourd and amaranth. In the lower levels of the Bat Cave, in New Mexico, dated to between 3600 and 2000 B.C., there were primitive corn-cobs, rinds of gourds, pumpkin seeds and rinds, and particles of sunflowers. In addition to these four centres described by MacNeish there may well be a fifth centre of early American agriculture in the south American tropical forest where such crops as bitter and sweet manioc, and the yam, were experimented with and domesticated perhaps even before 1000 B.C. – in lowland Venezuela possibly earlier still and maybe as far back as 2000 B.C.[104]

The agriculture that developed in these areas produced from such beginnings settled villages growing in size and complexity. In Peru from 750 B.C. onwards, the Formative period saw the rise of truly permanent villages often associated with large centres having temples on platforms. There were, quite naturally, variants in the various regional cultural groups that make up the Formative period of Peru, but there is a clear, over-all, general pattern: the villages are small and few, the agriculture includes maize, but probably not canal irrigation, the arts of pottery and stone-carving are good, and there develops a particularly fine art style, that of Chavín, named after the site of Chavín de Huantar. Earth and stone or adobe pyramids and other ceremonial buildings were started at this time – the last three-quarters of the first millennium B.C.

Towards the end of the Chavín period of the Formative in Peru, Chavín art disappears, new food plants appear and canal irrigation begins. The Classic cultures of Peru now take shape: the prehistoric Peruvian civilizations have various names and subdivisions which need not concern us here too much – for example the late Gallinazo-Mochica phase of the North Coast, the Maranga of the Central Coast, the Nazca of the South Coast, the Recnay and Cajamaran II and III of the northern Highland, and the Classic Tiahuanaco and probably the Pucara of the southern Highland.

It used to be said that this early Peruvian civilization – this civilization of the Classic phase – belonged to the second half of the first millennium A.D., but C14 dates now suggest that it goes back to the beginning of the Christian era, and some suggest even earlier. Professor Michael Coe thinks that civilization in Peru may well have started as early as the eighth century B.C.[105]

The general characteristics of the ancient Peruvian civilization are easy to list. These are: (1) massive flat-topped adobe pyramids and palace complexes; (2) three-dimensional or modelled art – as shown so well in the Mochica and Nazca pottery [Plates 71–5]; (3) metallurgy, which had begun in Chavín times but now developed to include casting, alloying, annealing, soldering in bronze, copper and gold, gilding and the manufacture of copper weapons and helmets; (4) textile working; (5) in the highlands, a fine stone architecture such as the temple of Pucara, the Calassaya enclosure, and, perhaps best known of all, the great monolithic gateway and stairway at Tiahuanaco; (6) large buildings with rooms, corridors, and courtyards, usually in conjunction with or near great pyramids, and these large buildings are usually interpreted as palaces or special public or even governmental buildings; (7) and lastly, large populations grouped around the pyramid or temple centres. The so-called Gallinazo III phase had huge pyramid mounds, and the late town here consisted of thirty thousand adobe-walled rooms around the pyramid in the Viru valley.

We have said that some people deny the label civilization to the Classic phase in America, but I agree with Americanists in general that the Peruvian Classic phase is civilization. Admittedly, of the attributes which we listed as characteristic of the civilizations of the Old World, one is here lacking: there is no writing. The Incas, whom the conquistadors met, belong to the last and post-Classic stage in Peru. The Inca period, and this is a period of empire and not primary civilization, is from about A.D. 1000 to 1532. The cities of the earlier civilization were places that had grown up as clusters around a temple centre. The Inca cities were planned, or at least partially planned, in their layout [Plate 68]. The Incas, as we have already said, did not have writing in any proper sense of that word. They relied on a mnemonic device of knotted strings – the *quipu* – which was, as Gelb has said, only suitable for 'rudimentary accounting purposes'.[106]

Let us now turn from Peru to the other early centre of civilization in Nuclear America – Mexico. Armillas has summarized the four stages of development in Mexico; first, the beginnings of plant domestication with cultivated plants as a mere addition to an economy still primarily based on the gathering of wild plants with supplementary hunting; then, as a second stage, there was a shift to an economy in which established farming formed the basis of subsistence and the spread of settled village farming communities; thirdly, the development of the high culture, or, in Redfield's terms, the growth of the great tradition, as distinct from the little or folk tradition. It is this growth that marks the threshold of civilization, and the fourth stage is represented by the rise of urban communities.

Village life and the making of pottery seem to have begun in Mexico about 2000 B.C. About the middle of the first millennium B.C., the Mexican synoecism is happening. From the beginning of the millennium developments from the small villages take place: the large cemetery of Tlatilco in the western suburbs of Mexico City dates from *c.* 1000 to 500 B.C., but its corresponding settlement is not known. As the first millennium was nearing its end Teotihuacán

[Plate 64] and Monte Albán [Plates 66–7] become the metropolises of the Valley of Mexico and of Central Oaxaca respectively. They are the earliest urban centres in Mexico, but behind them lay the first civilization of Mesoamerica, the civilization of the Olmecs.

This most ancient civilization of Mexico flourished in the sweltering Gulf Coast plain in the region of southern Veracruz and neighbouring Tabasco – to the west of the area of the Maya. It has been known for some while because of its remarkable jade objects and sculptures, many emphasizing human infants with snarling, jaguar-like features [Plates 60–62]. For some while the date of the Olmec people was in dispute: Mexican archaeologists argued for an early date but North American archaeologists were inclined to a date between A.D. 300 and 900. We now know that the Mexicans were right: C14 dates at the site of La Venta show that the Olmec civilization flourished from 800 to 400 B.C. 'There is now not the slightest doubt,' writes Michael Coe, 'that all later civilizations in Mesoamerica, whether Mexican or Mayan, ultimately rest on an Olmec base.'[107]

The Olmec heartland was an area only 125 miles long by 50 miles wide. It is a region of very high annual rainfall, a high-lying tropical forest, and a great deal of swampy lowland. This is indeed an inhospitable environment and one that is very different from the environments of the Old World civilizations of Egypt, Mesopotamia, India and China. La Venta was a ceremonial or élite centre which, according to Heizer, must have been supported by a population of some eighteen thousand persons; the main pyramid took some eight hundred thousand man-days to construct. Tres Zapotes lies a hundred miles north-west of La Venta; between them is the site of San Lorenzo, famous for its colossal stone heads, one of them 9 feet 4 inches high [Plate 57].

The Olmec art style is strange, and gives us an insight into a curious religion. The Olmecs believed that in the past a woman and a jaguar were matched, and that as a result of this there arose a race or species of were-jaguars. These obsess Olmec art: they are fat and sexless [Plates 57–63]. The Olmec people were great stone carvers; not only did they make massive heads but also small jade objects like axes, pendants and figurines. Olmec objects bear hieroglyphs which are at present unreadable but appear to be in part ancestral to some of the Maya glyphs. Here, then, we have the beginning of writing in Mexico, in the middle Formative period between 1000 and 300 B.C. Tres Zapotes produced the oldest dated monument in the New World: Stela C, a fragmentary basalt monument re-used in later times. The Olmecs were not a peaceful people. They had war clubs and individuals carried a kind of cestus or knuckle-duster.

The Olmec area, as we have seen, is in the north on the shores of the Gulf of Mexico. Another comparable civilization or high culture arose at about the same time in southern Mexico, in the Valley of Oaxaca, and Monte Albán is the most important site of this southern group [Plates 66–7]. It is in the centre of the country now occupied by people who speak a Zapotec language, and it has seemed reasonable to call it the Zapotec civilization. Most of Monte Albán dates from Classic times but Monte Albán I is *c.* 300 B.C. This early Zapotec civilization may well be derived directly from the Olmecs of the north; but whereas there is little evidence for writing and the calendar in the Olmec area, there is plenty of evidence in south Mexico. The first literary texts in Mexico come from Monte Albán I.[108]

The development of civilization in Mesoamerica was not, then, confined to one region: in addition to the Olmec region of Tabasco, the Zapotec region of Oaxaca, there were the Valley of Mexico and the Highlands and Lowlands of the Maya area. By the beginning of the Christian era there stood in the Valley of Mexico the site of Teotihuacán – the word means the House of the Gods. It is in a side pocket of the Valley of Mexico, in a dry valley twenty-five miles north-east of Mexico City. It was the greatest city of pre-Columbian America, no less than a Central Mexican metropolis with wide trading relations. It covered an area of more than three square miles and was fully urbanized with a gridded layout [Plate 64]; it contained great palaces and famous temples and pyramids like the Pyramid of the Sun, and of the Moon. The city had a population which grew from ten thousand to a possible maximum of one hundred and twenty thousand. The Pyramid of the Sun at Teotihuacán is one of the largest pre-Spanish structures in Mesoamerica. It is 700 feet long by 200 feet high: a high straw roof once crowned the summit.[109]

The period A.D. 300 to 900, a time which corresponds in Great Britain to the end of Roman power and the growth of the Anglo-Saxon and Celtic kingdoms, is in Central America the period of the flourishing of the great Mexican civilization – it has often been called and with reason the Golden Age of Mexico. This classic civilization of Mexico was literate: most people possessed books, and dates were recorded. The economy was based on the trinity of maize, beans and squash; but it was a simple farming economy, and there was no irrigation. The technology was a 'neo-lithic' one involving obsidian chipping of great skill for the manufacture of spearheads and dart-points and large quantities of razor blades. Metals were unknown until after A.D. 900 and so the vast buildings decorated with elaborate and beautiful frescoes were entirely done by stone carving and cutting. The Classic Mexican religion involved a pantheon of gods in a confusing and splendid variety: the main one was the Rain God, Tlaloc, metamorphosed out of the Olmec were-jaguar; besides his consort, the Water-Goddess, other leading deities were the Sun-God, the Moon-Goddess, and the Feathered Serpent, known later as Quetzalcoatl.

The civilization of Teotihuacán and its city came to an end about A.D. 600, an end in part caused perhaps by the destruction of the surrounding forests, in part by unknown invaders. The rulers of Mexico in the time of the conquistadors were of course the Aztecs, and even in late Aztec times Moctezuma II frequently made pilgrimages on foot to the ruins of Teotihuacán.

The last of the four Mesoamerican proto-historic civilizations was that of the Maya of south-east Mexico. They have been called the Greeks of the New World, and in their achievements they certainly outstripped other American pre-Columbian high cultures. The first Maya centres were established between 500 B.C. and A.D. 300; the Classic Maya period is from A.D. 300 to 900 – the period of the Old Empire: the New Empire was established *c*. A.D. 1000 and lasted until the arrival of the Spaniards. The most ancient Maya date is on a stela from Tikal dated A.D. 292. The most famous Maya sites are Chichen Itzá [Plate 65], Tikal, Uaxactun, Copán and Palenque.

The agriculture of the Maya centred on maize, which they regarded as the greatest gift of the gods – in fact a god itself. The Mayan way of life seemed to consist of people living in dispersed rural hamlets while only a small élite of priests and officials permanently inhabited the religious centres. Their sanctuaries are found in the forested area of the lowlands of Guatemala and the adjacent countries, the

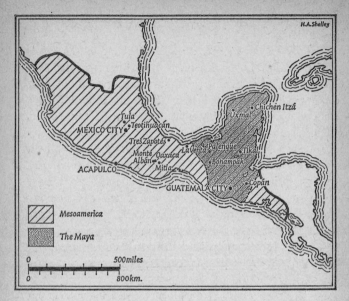

Figure 15. Mesoamerica and the Maya region

uplands of Chiapas and British Honduras and the Yucatán peninsula. The Maya have been described as a civilization without cities. From the beginning of agriculture in Peru there were sizeable communities – villages of a few hundred inhabitants with a temple centre and other communal buildings, in addition to hamlets around. But, on the present evidence, it seems that the nucleated dwelling centre did not enter into the Maya way of life. The hamlets were at a distance from the centre with its monumental ball-court, carved stelae, writing and evidence of skill in the arts. Yet these ceremonial centres could be defined as cities in the widest sense of the word. Bushnell describes them as not really cities but rather more like cathedral closes, the priests, attendants and officials supported by the peasants living in the hamlets around.

The Mayan ceremonial centres were not in defensible positions and they were not fortified. Each centre, ruled over by one or more priests, seems to have maintained amicable relations with the rulers of the other centres. The centres consisted of courts, platforms and pyramids. The Mayan religious ceremonies involved prayer, dancing, sacrifice, feasting and incense-burning. Men made offerings of their own blood drawn from the ears, the tongue [Plate 76] and elsewhere using aloe thorns sometimes attached to a string. The great ceremonies had music from trumpets, rattles and drums. Human sacrifice was comparatively rare, but in post-Classic times when new influences arrived from Central Mexico, the Mayan ceremonial ball-game became associated with human sacrifice, and a member of a losing team might have his head cut off by the winners.

The great achievement of the Maya was the knowledge of mathematics and astronomy; they had a complex calendar and knew the length of the solar year with great accuracy.

The Maya carved hieroglyphic inscriptions which are so well seen in their ceremonial centres; they were almost all concerned with the passage of time under the aegis of the appropriate gods. The same hieroglyphic writing was painted on strips of bark-cloth sized with lime; three books of such strips survive, the so-called *Codices*. The decipherment, at least in part, of the Maya hieroglyphs has been helped by the survival of several Maya dialects as spoken languages to the present day and the records left by Spaniards like Bishop Diego de Landa in the middle of the sixteenth century. Many glyphs still evade decipherment, but much has been read. Coe says: 'We are a long way from "cracking" the Maya script, but it seems that the way has been shown.'[110]

The Maya had a low level of agricultural techniques. They had no draught animals and no plough: they grew their maize in *milpas*, clearings in the jungle. After a few years the weeds and the exhaustion of the soil made them move to a new *milpa*, which they cleared with stone axes and by burning. Many geographical reasons have been given for the end of the Maya civilization: erosion, the silting-up of the fresh water source and the replacement of the forest by uncultivable savanna in the course of the slash-and-burn *milpa* system. But most scholars see the end of the Maya in historical terms. A. V. Kidder refers to the decapitation of Maya society, and Eric Thompson says it was due to the collapse of at least the elaborate ceremonial life in purely historical terms.[111] But of course as people the Maya have not disappeared: there are still two million of them living in Yucatán, Guatemala, British Honduras, parts of the Mexican states of Tabasco and Chiapas and the western portions of Honduras and El Salvador.

In the New World in general, apart from the Maya, the growth of civilization was cut off by the Spanish conquest at a point which Adams has approximated as functionally equivalent to the Old Kingdom in Egypt or the Dynasty of Agade in Mesopotamia.[112]

As we have said on several occasions in this book, we are not concerned with the process of growth or the end of the old civilizations of the Old and New Worlds: we are trying to trace their origins through the medium of archaeology, and archaeological research in America in the last quarter of a century has shown a largely independent origin of civilization in several centres in Nuclear America – Peru, the Olmec-Zapotec-Valley of Mexico areas of Mexico, and

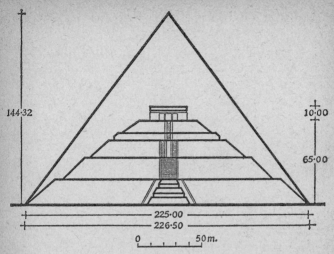

144·32

10·00

65·00

225·00
226·50

0   50 m.

Figure 16. Comparative elevations of the Pyramid of Kheops, Egypt, and the stepped Pyramid of the Sun, Teotihuacán, Mexico.

the Maya area. Most Americanists now agree with Willey when he says that the American civilizations stand 'clearly apart and essentially independent from the comparable culture core of the Old World'.

What is particularly fascinating about the ancient civilizations of America is that their pattern in detail differs in so many ways from the pattern of those of the Old World. Let us, in concluding this chapter, list some of the remarkable differences. In the first place their tools and weapons were mainly of wood or of stone, and they utilized obsidian a great deal. Occasionally they had tools of copper: and bronze-working had begun before the Spanish conquest. But they really had no hard metals and certainly no iron. In an age of stone, or at best, a Chalcolithic age, they achieved remarkable buildings and remarkable sculptures. Secondly, they did not use the wheel, either in vehicles or in the making of pottery; and yet they had a few diminutive toys which were wheeled. Their basic economy was agricultural. They hunted and caught birds and were fishers, although their techniques of fishing were limited. Their agriculture consisted of growing seed plants like maize and beans and squashes, or planting tubers like cassava in Brazil and the West Indies and potatoes in the Andes. Yet, though agriculture was the basis of their lives, they had no ploughs: they used the digging stick and the hoe and had no draft animals. New World agriculture did not involve stock-breeding or the use of milk, or of dung fertilizer. The only beast of burden was the llama, which was confined to the highlands of the Andes, and is, in any case, small and said to be inefficient. Their transport was by canoe, reed rafts and the backs of men. The total list of domesticated animals in the New World civilizations is very small – apart from the llama, only turkeys, the so-called 'muscovy' duck, a small edible dog, and guinea-pigs. These civilizations, or some of them, had writing: that of the Aztecs was never developed beyond a fairly crude pictographic level, that of the Maya was used within narrow religious and astronomical contexts, while the Incas had only the *quipu*.

There is a great fascination in seeing how civilizations developed independently in the Old and New Worlds, with certain basic elements in common, but with a great variety in the detail of their cultural traits.

CHAPTER EIGHT

ARCHAEOLOGY AND THE ORIGINS OF CIVILIZATION

In this final chapter we come to the end of our inquiry into the light which archaeology throws on the origins of civilization. We have described briefly the discovery of the first seven civilizations – the civilizations of Sumer, Egypt, the Indus Valley, Shang China, Mexico, the Maya, and Peru.

I have described these seven civilizations as the 'first' because they were the earliest civilizations in the Old and New Worlds. In the foregoing chapters I have set out a necessarily bald, brief and superficial account of their characteristics, their distinguishing features, their styles, their differences. Our purpose, though, has been to study their origins, and in this last chapter we are back to our basic problem, or our series of basic problems. How did these civilizations come into existence? What does archaeology, our only source for these pre-literate pre-historic periods, tell us, or incline us to believe, about the origins of these civilizations, and, therefore about the origin of civilization itself?

We discussed in the first chapter the definitions of civilization, and I still think that the late Clyde Kluckhohn's crisp definition (see page 31) is the most useful and workable. A society to be called civilization, he said, must have two of the following three things: towns of more than 5,000 inhabitants, writing, and complex ceremonial centres. If we accept this definition, then our seven societies are civilized, although it is to be remembered that the Maya may have had no cities in the Sumerian and Indus Valley sense of this word, and that perhaps the Egyptians until dynasty XVIII had no cities – though this will I think be proved to be wrong and the early dynastic Egyptian cities will be discovered – and the Incas, with their cities and complex organization, were a civilization without writing.

The first question which the intelligent reader of this book will ask is this: Has the author in writing it, or in giving the lectures on which it is based, made a personal and arbitrary selection of the ancient civilizations of the past? Why is there here no mention of Crete and the Hittites and Jericho and Mycenae? There are Maya but no Minoans: Why? The answer to this question is twofold. Jericho revealed a developing culture, even at times perhaps a high culture in the American sense of the Formative; and so did Çatal Hüyük. Neither Jericho nor Çatal Hüyük were civilizations: they were large settlements that could be called towns or proto-towns. They did not have the other requirements of the Kluckhohn formula. They may have been unsuccessful experiments towards civilization, a synoecism that did not succeed; or we might label them just as very overgrown peasant villages.[113]

So much for Jericho and Çatal Hüyük. Knossos and Mycenae and the Hittites call for a very different answer. And this is, that all these came later. Knossos was, as we all know, earlier than Anyang and the Olmecs, Zapotecs and Maya, but it was later than Egypt and Sumer among the Old World civilizations. It may have been a comparable or parallel experiment in the growth of society, but the Minoan civilization was an experiment that was being repeated within the known contexts of civilization as an already essayed and tried form of human society in the most ancient Near East. It may have been another experiment or it may have been a transplantation from elsewhere: that is not our concern here – our concern is with the first civilized societies. We are investigating the first experiments in civilization, the first essays in literate city existence; and once we know how those first experiments happened we can turn to the later civilizations and examine their birth and growth with a new, experienced and sure eye.

Because – and I purposely reiterate – the others are repeating the experiment. The synoecism in Greece which Thucydides described was an experiment which was repeated *de nova* there; the villages grew and grouped round one of their number which turned into a city and the group became a city-state. This was not a copy of what took place earlier in Egypt or Mesopotamia; it was not ordained by invaders coming with a higher culture from outside. It happened, and it happened because of social, political and economic forces within the Greek community.[114]

So it is not Greece or Mycenae or Knossos that we have wanted to study here: that is a study for other people at other times. Our study is the beginning of synoecism – the first experiments in civilization. That is the reason why we have been concerned only with seven early civilizations.

A second very common and very pertinent question is this: Granted that you have not merely made a selection of early civilizations, why should we suppose at this moment of time that we have at our disposal a complete roster of early civilizations? May it not be that others will be discovered, perhaps in the next decade, certainly in the next half century, which will render invalid what is being said now? This is a very sensible query. Let us remember that the prehistoric Indus civilization was discovered only in the first years of the second decade of this century, that the civilization of Anyang/Shang China was discovered archaeologically only in 1928, and that our knowledge of the Olmec and Zapotec civilizations of Mexico and of the development of early Peruvian civilization is very recent indeed. Let us face this question fairly and squarely: in 1920, anyone writing about the problem we are now discussing would confine himself to Egypt, Sumer and the Maya. It is obvious that our picture of early civilization changes enormously with the progress of archaeological discovery – and archaeological discovery continues vigorously and relentlessly from year to year. Why should we know the complete picture in the mid-sixties when we did not do so in 1920?

What additional early civilizations shall we know about in forty years time, and how will they affect our general theoretical picture of man's ancient past and his development from barbarism into civilized living? There may well exist early civilizations other than those we have described, but, surely, if there were a hint of them, and a suggestion of areas in which they could be most propitiously looked for, the resources of our many wealthy research foundations and grant-giving bodies in Europe and America would have been harnessed to finding them. The real answer to this problem is that there is at the moment no obvious place to look: the Amazonian forest perhaps, the Congo, Abyssinia, the forests of Cambodia, the Ganges valley, Afghanistan, south central Russia? There could have been early civilizations in one or other of these areas: we do not know, but we do live in an age of countless travellers and countless archaeological expeditions. It is fair to say that one does not hear gossip about mysterious hitherto unknown cities of the remote past: the lost cities and the vanished civilizations about which our travellers and popularizing archaeologists write are those we know about, or often enough those of medieval and later historical times.

Clearly the past, the remote past of man which we have

here been studying, has a future; but it should not frighten us any more, indeed much less than the future of the present. Our task at the moment is to try to understand the past as it appears at present. Our real problem is to answer this question: How can we in the sixties of the twentieth century describe the origins of civilization in terms differing from John Lubbock in his *Origins of Civilization* a hundred years ago? There is no doubt about the first part of the answer to this question. We can now reaffirm the great change in human history which Elliot Smith insisted on in his book with that very title, *Human History*, first published in 1930. This was the change from man the food-gatherer and hunter to man the agriculturist and breeder of animals; the change from man, using his environment but still enslaved by it, to man who both controlled his environment and could be at least in part responsible for his food supply.

Elliot Smith called this the Food Producing Revolution; Gordon Childe equated it with the Neolithic of the Lubbock Four-Age version of the Thomsen Three-Age system, and introduced the perhaps unhappy phrase 'the Neolithic Revolution' into archaeological and historical writing. It was unhappy, or it seems unhappy now, for three reasons: first, it equates the change from food-gathering to food-producing with the change from chipped stone implements to polished stone implements. Lubbock's 'Neolithic' was defined by four cultural traits – pottery, polished stone implements, agriculture and domesticated animals. We know now that this quadrilogy is not something that happened always at the same time; but because we have in archaeology retained some of the old terminology, we now hear archaeologists speaking of the non-ceramic Neolithic or the aceramic Neolithic, when all they mean is that they have found traces of early food-producing communities whose technology does not however include the making of pottery.

In the second place, the phrase 'revolution' suggests to most ordinary people something that happened violently, whereas the more we learn about the transition from food-gathering to food-producing in the Old and the New World, the more clearly do we appreciate that this was a long and slow process of experimentation and development. No doubt some of the experiments failed: we only know the successes with domesticates which appear in the archaeological record. It is certainly not to be supposed that we know as yet all the successful experiments that have happened; we may not know them for many a long period.

I have said 'experiments' deliberately because here is the third unsatisfactory feature of Childe's 'Neolithic Revolution'. He thought of it as something that happened in one place at one time – in the most ancient Near East. We have only in the last ten years – so quickly does new archaeological knowledge accumulate – realized that the ancient Near East (or south-west Asia and Egypt) was only one centre of the domestication of plants and animals; and that also in this one centre, extending from western Anatolia to Iran and from the Zagros Mountains to Egypt and Mesopotamia, there may have been many centres of domestication. Quite apart from that, it is arguable and likely that crops were domesticated in China long before any knowledge of wheat came to China from the West. And, in Nuclear America, four or five groups domesticated various crops quite independently of the Old World, and perhaps independently of each other. Moreover, there is no reason to suppose that we have as yet found all the evidence of the early domesticates and all the incipient agricultural societies. There could have been an early agriculture based on rice in south China or the Ganges; and it has been argued that a sorghum millet domestication might have happened independently in Nigeria. And let us also not forget that Abyssinia has been suggested as one of the possible centres of early agriculture.[115]

Our main concern throughout this book is with the next stage in human history, the stage which Childe called the Urban Revolution. Elliot Smith and Perry were certain and outspoken about the nature of the change from peasant village communities to civilization. They insisted that this took place once and once only, and that it took place in Egypt: to them and their school, civilization started in Egypt and was diffused from there to Mesopotamia and the Indus Valley and to China – and even further, across the Pacific to Central America.[116] We have already mentioned the Egypt-in-America thesis: no reasonable archaeologist or anthropologist at the present day sees any Egyptian influence in the Central American civilizations, while not of course denying the possibility of external stimuli.[117]

But is it possible to believe in a modified version of the Elliot Smith/Perry theory? If any Egyptian origin for the civilizations of the New World is no longer arguable, is it still possible that all the Old World civilizations are derived from Egypt? Most people at present think not, and it is surely indisputable that the Sumerian civilization was earlier than that of the Egyptians. Could we then not transfer the hyper-diffusionist theory from the banks of the Nile to those of the Tigris-Euphrates? This is precisely what Lord Raglan did in his *How Came Civilization?* In that book he made all civilization come from southern Mesopotamia, and it is to be remembered that, as Kramer put it, Sumer did have a large number of 'firsts' in human history. Raglan's philosophy of the origins of civilization is based on this impressive list of firsts, but also on the unthinkable conviction that nothing could be invented more than once. Raglan laid it down as a principle that the savage never invented anything, and it is in this assertion that we may see the impossibility of accepting the hyper-diffusionist school of thought. Because, in the first place, the savage did invent many things: agriculture for example and the domestication of animals; and, as we now believe, he invented these patterns of food production in several different parts of the world. The barbarian agriculturist farmer whom the savage created and invented, went further, and – here we agree with Raglan – invented civilization in southern Mesopotamia. So it is no longer any use saying that the savage invented nothing and the barbarian invented nothing: we should not be here in the twentieth century A.D. lecturing to students in universities and writing books if it had not been for the long succession of inventive savages and barbarians who lived centuries before us.[118]

And it is just not true to say that things cannot be discovered or invented more than once; it is nonsense and results from a refusal to study the history of invention and discovery in all realms – prehistory, ethnology, and history itself. Darwin and Wallace are good examples of parallel development in the realm of ideas. It is equally at variance with the facts to say that stray cultural contacts cannot occur, and that ideas and techniques cannot be diffused in a simple and individual way. Dr Joseph Needham has pointed out that historically we have excellent examples of the diffusion of mechanical and other techniques from China to the west – the compass, for instance, paper, printing blocks, and the crossbow. If these came from the east to the west, then we should not boggle at the possibility in earlier times of wheat-growing, the alloying of copper and tin to make bronze, and the *cire-perdue* process of bronze-casting coming from west to east, or rather from the most ancient Near East to China.[119]

It may be thought that in talking of the Elliot Smith pan-Egyptian theory and the Raglan pan-Sumerian theory we are tilting at a past generation of archaeologists and anthropologists, but hyper-diffusionists are still with us. The monogenetic theory of cultural origins and the hyper-diffusionist model of thought is not dead. Professor Heine-Geldern still argues that all civilization originated in the Near East; among other things he bases this on the spread of writing and argues that all scripts can be traced back to a people with grey or black polished pottery who lived in eastern Asia Minor and expanded from that region in many directions in the second half of the fourth millennium B.C.[120] We cannot avoid a word of sympathy for people like Elliot Smith, Perry, Raglan and Heine-Geldern: they have all wanted a simple universal answer to a very complex problem, and how much easier is their answer than the sort of answer we have been hinting at, namely independent synoecisms with stimulus-diffusion and cultural borrowings. And we must not reject a simple solution if it seems to fit the facts: but the single origin of civilization is not a simple solution – it is a simplistic one.

And a simplistic historical answer is no better, and no worse, than a simplistic geographical answer. It seems fairly easy and obvious to say that in the Old World the first four civilizations developed in river valleys, but one still asks why; one also asks why there are not comparable civilizations in other river valleys such as the Ganges, the Irrawaddy, the Mekong, the Congo and the Amazon. Moreover, if it is just great river valleys that gave rise to early civilization, we must ask why it is that it was only in certain river valleys that this happened? And when we look at Nuclear America we see three civilizations that cannot possibly be said to have arisen in comparable environments to those of the four Old World civilizations. Indeed the heights of Peru, the central valley of Mexico and the Gulf Coast, in themselves three very varied environments, cannot possibly be usefully compared with the four great river valleys that were the environment of the Old World civilizations.

If there is not a single historical or geographical factor to explain the origin of civilization, is there a single technological factor? This has been suggested; it has been argued that it was irrigation with its necessity for organization and the creation of a complicated society, that brought civilization into existence. Developing village societies who had to group together and plan great works, had then to group together in other ways which created an urban literate life. In a word, synoecism was a process thrust on developing agricultural villages by irrigation.

We have, then, three simple theories to explain the origin of civilization: first, the historical theory, that all was the result of diffusion from one centre where the miracle of civilization occurred once, and once only, in human history; secondly, the geographical theory, that it was a particular environment – river valleys – that caused this great jump forward in human culture; and thirdly, that a particular aspect of technology, perhaps irrigation, promoted it.

In November 1962, the William March Rice University in the United States of America held a symposium entitled 'Prehistoric Man in the New World', which formed part of the celebration of the fiftieth year since the opening of that University. Lengthier versions of the papers given in this symposium were published in 1964 in a large and important volume with the same title, a volume which provides an up-to-date summary of our knowledge of pre-Columbian America. Dr Geoffrey Bushnell reviewed the book in *Antiquity*, and this was the last sentence of his review: 'Some deductions from the symposium lead up to thoughts on whether civilization arose once or more in the Old World, once or more in the New World, or perhaps once in the whole World.'[121]

And in that sentence, brought out into the open clearly and succinctly, is the issue we have been discussing in this book. As far as the Old World is concerned I hope we now feel that we know the answer, namely that the first civilization happened in Mesopotamia, and that an independent process of synoecism occurred in Egypt and the Indus Valley, both stimulated from Sumer. China was a more difficult problem, but it does seem to be an example of the independent invention of agriculture and the independent invention of civilization, although there was a contact and borrowing from the West. We must distinguish between the contact and borrowing that affected the growth of culture in China, and the stimulus-diffusion that affected the synoecisms of Egypt and the Indus Valley.

Indeed it is China and the New World that really put our general problem into its sharpest perspective. If we do not think clearly about the origins of urban literate life in China and Nuclear America, we shall perhaps deceive ourselves about the whole issue in general. Let us now concentrate on Nuclear America. We have argued that the early American civilizations came into existence by their own process of synoecism. In describing the rise of the Olmecs, the Maya, the Classic civilization of ancient Peru, we are not prepared to see any alien civilization colonizing America – Egyptians, Jaredites, Phoenicians, lost tribes of Israel, inhabitants of Atlantis or Mu, or what you will. But it is one thing to reject, as the archaeological and ethnological evidence tells us to reject, the idea of civilization coming to America from outside; it is quite another thing to deny the possibility of influences coming to America from outside.

Japanese sailors have been shipwrecked and blown into the harbour of San Francisco. Ekholm has written convincingly on this matter. 'Winds and currents', he writes, 'have caused many a disabled Chinese junk to be driven on to our Pacific shore', and adds that it is 'conceivable that survivors might have found their way back to the Far East and instigated subsequent travel'. Ekholm considers it likely that 'small groups of persons (boatloads if you like) landed at different places and moved inland to some of the main cultural centres'.

And we must remember that this sort of thing could have happened without necessarily leaving any precise or tangible witness in the archaeological record. But some evidence for precise and exact parallels has been accumulated in recent years. Ekholm himself has emphasized the close resemblance between the wheeled toys of Central America, and Asiatic examples, and it is curious that whereas the pre-Columbian people of some parts of America had wheeled toys, the wheel was not used by them for pottery-making and for carts. Then Betty Meggers, Clifford Evans and Emilio Estrada have emphasized the appearance of pottery on the coast of Ecuador which they find exactly paralleled in the Jōmon Neolithic of Japan.[122]

These contacts need not be denied, and the complete absence of trans-Pacific stimuli for cultural developments in the New World need not be insisted upon dogmatically. Contacts and stimuli could have happened, but most present-day Americanists view them with doubt. There is nowadays no suggestion of any direct transplantation of an Old World civilization to the New, and indeed no suggestion of Old World-New World contacts comparable to the Mesopotamian–Egyptian catalysis we have discussed. Any contacts trans-Atlantic or trans-Pacific that may have occurred were slight and very infrequent and had little effect on the native development of pre-Columbian American culture.[123]

The nineteenth-century archaeologists and anthropologists spent a great deal of their time arguing whether independent evolution or diffusion was the explanation of human cultural change and development. One of the most thoughtful and important studies of the theoretical basis of our thinking on these matters is provided by Professor Julian Steward in his *Theory of Cultural Change*. Steward makes the point that even when diffusion as a fact has been demonstrated between two cultural traditions, it by itself is insufficient to 'explain' their likenesses. 'One may fairly ask', he says, 'whether each time a society accepts diffused culture it is not an independent recurrence of cause and effect,' an arresting and helpful idea. Steward himself rejects the principle of unilinear cultural evolution maintained by Tylor, Lewis H. Morgan, and now in part by Willey and Phillips – a doctrine which says that all human culture passes historically through similar developmental stages. Steward propounds a multilinear evolutionary theory according to which all peoples do not pass automatically through similar stages, but a finite number of parallel evolutions take place – not natural laws but regularities or generalizations of limited range.[124]

When discussing Steward's views, Professor R. McC. Adams said that it was now 'possible to regard all four areas as historically distinct examples regardless of the ultimate "origins" of particular traits', and the four areas he was referring to were Mesopotamia, Egypt, pre-Spanish

Mesoamerica and Peru. If he had included the civilizations of the Indus and the Yellow River he would have got to six. I would separate out the Olmec-Zapotec civilization from that of the Maya, and so make seven – the seven ancient civilizations we have been discussing. And, to modify Adams's phrase, it now seems to me that these seven are historically distinct examples of the creation of civilizations, quite regardless of the ultimate origins of any particular traits such as bronze-casting in Shang China.

History begins at Sumer was the title of one of Kramer's books, and while it is true that the first civilization and the oldest written history was in southern Mesopotamia, I would prefer to say that civilization and history began seven times. Why? Because seven separate societies in a state of cultural development in which they were able to develop certain possibilities that, if used, could promote synoecism, accepted the challenge of those possibilities and became civilized.

But is this a good enough answer? Is it not a description of the process, the answer to how, rather than to why? The question we have been asking is why, and the answer here surely lies in the nature of man and culture. There is a supra-organic, a cultural evolution in man's development. Kroeber wrote in 1940: 'We must consider that civilization is an inevitable response to laws governing the growth of culture and controlling the man-culture relationship', and in his Preface to a book of essays entitled *New Paths to Yesterday*, Professor Caldwell says: 'Perhaps there is only a finite number of social and historical processes behind the events of history.'[125] I think Kroeber and Caldwell are right; the lesson of archaeology at the present day is, I suggest, that seven societies in seven different ways trod one of these paths, the path that led to civilization.

To say that it is inevitable, that civilization is inevitable, suggests that synoecism must happen everywhere; but French geographers are never tired of pointing out that still, at the present day, eighty per cent of the world's population live in villages, and Stuart Piggott, surveying the whole problem of human cultural development from the standpoint of an archaeologist and ancient historian, says that it is barbarism which is the norm of human society and civilization the exception.[126] This is an arguable point of view: our concern in this book has been to see how these exceptions first occurred in the history of man.

If I read the archaeological evidence aright, and much of the evidence relevant to our problem has come to light only in the last fifteen to twenty years, the diffusionist and most certainly the hyper-diffusionist model of the past is not now suitable, and the same applies to the unilinear evolutionary model of thought. We should now think in terms of multilinear evolution leading inevitably, as Kroeber said, for some societies with geographical and ecological and cultural possibilities, to synoecism – one of the finite number of social and historical processes behind the events of history.

In his *Origins of Civilization*, written a century ago, Sir John Lubbock wrote: 'I submit then that if some of the suggestions I throw out and the opinions I expressed in my early works have been criticized by great authorities, I am able to show that they are supported by others, and what, of course is of even more importance, they are in accordance with facts.' I believe that an interpretation of the origins of civilization in terms of multilinear evolution is in accordance with the archaeological facts as now known to us.

SEMINAR NOTES

CHAPTER I

1. Stuart Piggott, 'The Science of Rubbish', the *Spectator*, 9 April 1965, p. 482. Piggott was quoting a writer in the *Builder* of 1846, who said: 'That's Archaeology, mon cher, the Science of Rubbish.'

2. Sir Thomas Browne's *Religio Medici* (1642), chapter 5; Francis Bacon, *Advancement of Learning* (1605), Book II.

3. E. A. Hooton, *Apes, Men and Morons* (London, 1938), p. 218. Professor Hooton was, of course, here being a devil's advocate and goes on to say: 'Actually archaeology is quite as legitimate an inquiry into the past as is history. . . . Archaeology shares with history the function of interpreting the present through knowledge of the past.'

4. For an account of the methods of the archaeologist, see Grahame Clark, *Archaeology and Society* (3rd edn., London, 1957); Sir Mortimer Wheeler, *Archaeology from the Earth* (Oxford, 1954); Sir Leonard Woolley, *Digging up the Past* (Harmondsworth, Penguin Books, 1937); Stuart Piggott, *Approach to Archaeology* (London, 1959); Sigfried de Laet, *Archaeology and its Problems* (London, 1957); Frank Hole and Robert F. Heizer, *An Introduction to Prehistoric Archaeology* (New York, 1965).

5. My own professional interests can be seen by looking at G. E. Daniel, *The Prehistoric Chamber Tombs of England and Wales* (Cambridge, 1950), *The Prehistoric Chamber Tombs of France* (London, 1960) and *The Megalith Builders of Western Europe* (London, 1958).

6. That was in 1932. Recently a pupil of mine bought a copy of the 7th edition (published in 1913) from the current archaeological shelves of a bookshop in the West Country.

While the terms Palaeolothic and Neolithic were invented by Lubbock and first used in his *Prehistoric Times*, this book in 1865 was not the first moment when 'prehistory' was used. Daniel Wilson had used it in the title of his book *The Archaeological and Prehistoric Annals of Scotland* (first published in 1851) and Tournal was using it in 1833 – see R. F. Heizer, *Man's Discovery of his Past* (Englewood Cliffs, 1962, p. 79) and G. E. Daniel, *Origins and Growth of Archaeology* (Harmondsworth, Penguin Books, 1967, pp. 24–5).

7. For a critique of Toynbee see P. Geyl, 'Toynbee's System of Civilisations', *Journal of the History of Ideas*, 9, 1948, pp. 93–124; Toynbee's answer in *Med. der Kon. Nederlandse Akademie van Weterischappen afd. Letterkunde* (N.S. – 24), 1961, p. 7; P. Gourou, *Annales – Economies, Sociétés, Civilisations*, IV, 1959, pp. 445–50, and various essays and reviews by O. H. K. Spate conveniently collected together in his *Let Me Enjoy: Essays, partly Geographical* (London, 1966).

8. Ignacio Bernal in Jesse D. Jennings and Edward Norbeck (eds.), *Prehistoric Man in the New World* (Chicago, 1964), p. 562.

9. On the general problem of the origins of writing see David Diringer, *Writing* (London, 1962); I. J. Gelb, *A Study of Writing: the Foundations of Grammatology* (London, 1952); S. A. B. Mercer, *The Origin of Writing and our Alphabet* (London, 1959); and Maurice Pope, 'The Origin of Writing in the Near East', *Antiquity*, 1966, p. 17. It will be noted that Diringer doubts the invention of script in Mesopotamia (see his *The Alphabet*, New York, 1948, p. 41).

10. For a survey of the pre-literate societies of the world see Grahame Clark, *The Stone Age Hunters* (London, 1967); *World Prehistory, an Outline* (Cambridge, 1961); Grahame Clark and Stuart Piggott, *Prehistoric Societies* (London, 1965; revised editions London, and Harmondsworth, Penguin Books, 1970); K. P. Oakley, *Man, the Tool-Maker* (London, 5th edn., 1961).

11. For the transition between the pre-literate prehistoric period and the earliest literate civilizations see Clark and Piggott, *Pre-*

historic Societies (see previous note); Jacquetta Hawkes and Sir Leonard Woolley, *Prehistory and the Beginnings of Civilisation* (London, 1963); James Mellaart, *Earliest Civilizations of the Near East* (London, 1965).

12. A. L. Kroeber, *A Roster of Civilizations and Culture* (Chicago, 1962), p. 9.

13. For a different viewpoint see Arthur C. H. Bell, *Civilisation* (Harmondsworth, Penguin Books, 1938).

14. There has been a curious lack of interest in New World archaeology among Old World archaeologists until very recently. See *Antiquity*, 1967, p. 172.

15. Ralph Linton, *The Tree of Culture*, abridged by Adelin Linton (New York, 1959), p. 79.

16. Arthur Evans published his discoveries in Crete in an article in the *Monthly Review*, March, 1901, p. 115, which is reproduced in G. E. Daniel, *Origins and Growth of Archaeology* (Harmondsworth, Penguin Books, 1967), pp. 162–77.

17. Sir John Marshall in E. J. Rapson (ed.), *The Cambridge History of India*, Vol. I (Cambridge, 1922), p. 612.

18. For the discovery of Anyang see Li Chi and Liang Ssu-yung, *Preliminary Reports on Excavations at Anyang* (Peking and Nanking, 1929–33); H. G. Creel, *The Birth of China: A survey of the Formative Period of Chinese Civilisation* (London, 1936); and *Studies in Early Chinese Culture* (London, 1938).

19. For a discussion of Jericho, Crete, etc., in relation to the definition of the first civilizations see Chapter 8.

20. Childe's *Man Makes Himself* was first published in 1936 (London; also Harmondsworth, Penguin Books, 1942), and *What Happened in History* in 1942 (London). See also his *Progress and Archaeology* (London, 1944) and *Social Evolution* (London, 1951). For Redfield see *The Primitive World and its Transformations* (Chicago, 1941, and Harmondsworth, Penguin Books, 1968) and *Peasant Society and Culture* (Chicago, 1956).

21. These definitions are set out in Carl. H. Kraeling and Robert McC. Adams (eds.), *City Invincible: A Symposium on*

Urbanization and Cultural Development in the Ancient Near East (Chicago, 1960).

22. Stuart Piggott, Preface to M. E. L. Mallowan, *Early Mesopotamia and Iran* (London, 1965), p. 7.

23. The lake village on Lake Prasias is described in the *Histories* of Herodotus (Book V, 16). See Stanley Casson, *The Discovery of Man; The Story of the Inquiry into Human Origins* (London, 1959), pp. 46–7.

24. For an account of some of these 'barbarians' see T. Talbot Rice, *The Scythians* (London, 1957); T. G. E. Powell, *The Celts* (London, 1958); and *Prehistoric Art* (London, 1966).

25. This surprising phrase comes from *Locksley Hall* (line 168). A few lines in front is the phrase 'Knowledge comes, but wisdom lingers.'

26. *Archaeologia*, II, 1773, p. 241. Thomas Pownall was Lieutenant-Governor of New Jersey and later Governor of Massachusetts.

27. Sir E. B. Tylor (1832–1917), first Professor of Anthropology at Oxford, wrote his *Anthropology* in 1881. For an account of his work see R. R. Marett, *Tylor* (London, 1936).

28. Lewis H. Morgan's *Ancient Society* was reissued in 1964 (ed. Leslie A. White) as a volume in the John Harvard Library by the Belknap Press of the Harvard University Press.

29. On the development of the Three- and Four-Age system see G. E. Daniel, *The Three Ages* (Cambridge, 1943), and *A Hundred Years of Archaeology* (London, 1950).

30. For the marriage of models see Childe, *What Happened in History* (Harmondsworth, Penguin Books, 1942) and J. G. D. Clark, *From Savagery to Civilisation* (London, 1946).

31. For a discussion of American terminology see G. R. Willey and P. Phillips, *Method and Theory in American Archaeology* (Chicago, 1958).

32. On these techniques see F. E. Zeuner, *Dating the Past: an Introduction to Geochronology* (London, 4th edn., 1958).

33. On C14 dating see Willard F. Libby, *Radiocarbon Dating* (Chicago and London, 2nd edn., 1965).

34. For the absolute chronology of Palaeolithic art see H. L. Movius, 'Radiocarbon Dates and Upper Palaeolithic Archaeology', *Current Anthropology*, I, 1960, pp. 355–91.

35. See James Mellaart, *The Chalcolithic and Early Bronze Ages in the Near East and Anatolia* (Beirut, 1966) and *Earliest Civilizations of the Near East* (London, 1965).

36. Tylor's *Researches into the Early History of Mankind and the Development of Civilisation* was first published in 1865 and went through several printings. A new edition (called the third) was edited by Tylor himself in 1878. The most convenient modern edition is edited and abridged with an Introduction by Paul Bohannan (Chicago and London, 1964).

37. R. H. Lowie, *The History of Ethnological Theory* (London, 1937). This brilliant and penetrating study should be read by everyone interested in the nature of cultural change.

CHAPTER 2

38. *Genesis*, xi, verses 2 to 4. The wording of the Authorized Version is 'from the east'; the Revised Version says 'they journeyed east' or 'in the east'.

39. See H. Peake and H. J. Fleure, *Peasants and Potters* (Oxford, 1927), p. 42. This is volume III of the authors' series of which volume V is called *The Steppe and the Sown* (Oxford, 1928). The biblical quotation is: 'And Abel was a keeper of sheep, but Cain was a tiller of the ground' (*Genesis*, iv, 2). I always feel that it should have been Abel, the pastoral nomad from the steppe and desert, who murdered the peaceful agriculturist, and not the other way round. On the Flood story (*Genesis*, vii, viii) in relation to archaeology see A. Parrot, *The Flood and Noah's Ark* (London, 1955), and Sir Leonard Woolley in G. E. Daniel (ed.), *Myth or Legend?* (London, 1955), p. 39. Mesopotamia was the original home of the story in *Genesis* which is itself recorded in *The Epic of Gilgamesh*. Archbishop Ussher gave the precise date of the Flood as 2349 B.C.

40. On the geographical conditions in early Mesopotamia see Lees and Falcon, 'The Geographical History of the Mesopotamia Plain', *Geographical Journal*, 1942, p. 24.

41. The *Oxford English Dictionary* defines a Chaldean as 'a native of Chaldea, especially (as at Babylon) one skilled in occult learning, astrology, etc.' Rawlinson in his *Bampton Lectures*, V, p. 23 (1859) says: 'In *Daniel* the Chaldeans are a special set of persons at Babylon having a "learning" and a "tongue" of their own, and classed with the magicians, astrologers etc.' André Parrot in his *Sumer* (London, 1960) says that Chaldea was 'a name applied in the 19th century to Mesopotamia as a whole. It should be restricted to the area near the Persian Gulf and to the period of the first millennium B.C.'; and of the Chaldeans that this was 'a name incorrectly used in many books to designate the Sumerians. Stractly speaking it only applies to the tribes that settled Lower Mesopotamia in the 7th and 6th centuries B.C.' It is clearly unwise to use the words Chaldea and the Chaldeans at the present day.

42. On *tells* see P. Carleton, *Buried Empires* (London, 1939) and Seton Lloyd, *Mounds of the Near East* (Edinburgh, 1963).

43. For a good general account of cuneiform writing see E. Chiera, *They wrote on Clay: The Babylonian Tablets speak Today* (Cambridge, 1939).

44. On Grotefend see Seton Lloyd, *Foundations in the Dust* (London, 1947), pp. 78–9.

45. See Sir Wallis Budge, *The Rise and Progress of Assyriology* (London, 1925), and George Rawlinson, *A Memoir of Major-General Sir Henry Creswicke Rawlinson* (London, 1898), p. 146.

46. Sir Wallis Budge, *By Nile and Tigris* (London, 1920), I, p. 232.

47. The contributions of Edward Hincks (1792–1866) to the decipherment of hieroglyphics are mainly made in articles between 1833 and 1865 in the *Transactions of the Royal Irish Academy*.

48. Seton Lloyd, *Foundations in the Dust* (London, 1947), especially chapter 10.

49. The quotation is from W. K. Loftus, *Travel and Researches in Chaldea and Susiana* (London, 1857).

50. See especially his *Abraham* (London, 1935), *Ur of the Chaldees* (London, 1950), *Excavations at Ur* (London, 1954). The word Sumerology was being used in 1897. A. H. Sayce is in 1875 referring to Sumerians, but there were then two other spellings – namely, Sumirians and Shumerians.

51. M. E. L. Mallowan, *Early Mesopotamia and Iran* (London, 1965), p. 15.

CHAPTER 3

52. For general works on Sumer and the Sumerians see Mallowan's book already cited (note 51); V. G. Childe, *New Light on the Most Ancient East* (London, 1952); S. N. Kramer, *History begins at Sumer* (London, 1958) and *The Sumerians* (Chicago, 1963); A. Parrot, *Sumer* (London, 1960); G. Roux, *Ancient Iraq* (London, 1964 and Harmondsworth, Penguin Books, 1968).

53. J. Mellaart, *Çatal Hüyük* (London, 1967) and *Earliest Civilizations of the Near East* (London, 1963).

54. On the origins of metallurgy see R. J. Forbes, 'Extracting, Smelting, and Alloying' in Charles Singer, E. J. Holmyard, and A. R. Hall (eds.), *A History of Technology*, Vol. I (Oxford, 1954), p. 572.

55. For early wheels and wheeled vehicles see V. Gordon Childe, 'Wheeled Vehicles', in Singer, Holmyard, and Hall, (eds.), *A History of Technology* (see previous note), Vol. I, chapter 27.

56. Georges Roux, *Ancient Iraq* (London, 1964), p. 19.

57. The old idea of the quadrivium of the Neolithic is well set out in M. C. Burkitt, *Our Early Ancestors* (Cambridge, 1926). Read in conjunction with the following statement of Braidwood's in *City Invincible: A Symposium on Urbanization and*

Cultural Development in the Ancient Near East (Chicago, 1960), p. 308: 'If any definition of the "neolithic" were to be acceptable (though to me none would be, for the word has had too many meanings to regain precision), it would be in Childe's sense . . . of "a self-sufficing food-producing economy".'

58. On *synoecism* see G. Glotz, *The Greek City and its Institutions* (London, 1929), pp. 287, 288, 360 and elsewhere.

CHAPTER 4

59. On ancient Egypt see Cyril Aldred, *The Egyptians* (London, 1949), and *Egypt to the End of the Old Kingdom* (London 1965); I. E. S. Edwards, *The Pyramids of Egypt* (Harmondsworth, Penguin Books, 1961); *The Early Dynastic Period in Egypt* (fascicle 25 of the new *Cambridge Ancient History*, 1964); W. B. Emery, *Archaic Egypt* (Harmondsworth, Penguin Books, 1961).

60. For the geographical background of prehistoric and protohistoric Egypt see K. W. Butzer, *Physical Conditions in Eastern Europe, Western Asia, and Egypt before the Period of Agricultural and Urban Settlement* (fascicle 33 of the new *Cambridge Ancient History*, 1965).

61. On the Napoleonic campaign see J. Christopher Herold, *Bonaparte in Egypt* (London, 1963).

62. On hieroglyphs and the decipherment of the Rosetta Stone see Sir Alan Gardiner, *Egypt of the Pharaohs* (Oxford, 1961); Sir E. A. T. Wallis Budge, *The Rosetta Stone* (London, 10th revised edn., 1955); Sir Tomkyns Hilgrove Turner, *Archaeologia*, XVI, 1812, p. 212; J. F. Champollion, 'Lettre à M. Dacier relative à l'Alphabet des Hiéroglyphes Phonétiques', 1822 – these last two readily accessible in C. W. Ceram, *The World of Archaeology: The Pioneers tell their own Story* (London, 1966).

63. On the early chronology of dynastic Egypt see A. J. Arkell, 'Was King Scorpion Menes?', *Antiquity*, 1963, p. 31.

64. *Diospolis* was published in London in 1901. Petrie's dates were 1853 to 1942.

65. For the early Egyptian sites see Elise Baumgartel, *The Cultures of Prehistoric Egypt* (London, 1947); G. Caton Thompson and E. W. Gardner, *The Desert Fayum* (London, 1934); G. Brunton, *Mostagedda and the Tasian Culture* (London, 1937); G. Brunton and C. Caton Thompson, *The Badarian Civilization* (London, 1928).

66. Edgerton in *City Invincible* (see note 57), p. 144.

67. On the Gebel el-Arak knife handle see H. Frankfort, *The Birth of Civilisation in the Near East* (London, 1951).

68. See Frankfort, ibid., especially chapter 4, pp. 78–99, and Appendix, 'The Influence of Mesopotamia on Egypt towards the End of the Fourth Millennium B.C.'

69. Cyril Aldred, *Egypt to the End of the Old Kingdom* (see note 59), p. 36.

70. John A. Wilson in *City Invincible* (see note 57), and see also his *The Burden of Egypt* (Chicago, 1951).

71. For Butzer's views see K. W. Butzer, *Environment and Archaeology: An Introduction to Pleistocene Geography* (London, 1964), especially chapters 29, 30 and 31, and his fascicle in the new *Cambridge Ancient History* already cited (note 60).

72. See here P. Carleton, *Buried Empires* (London, 1939), pp. 137–40.

73. On race and racial classification see J. S. Huxley, A. C. Haddon, and A. M. Carr-Saunders, *We Europeans: A Survey of 'Racial' Problems* (London, 1935); William C. Boyd and Isaac Asimov, *Races and People* (London and New York, 1958); Ruth Benedict, *Race: Science and Politics* (New York, 4th edn., 1959).

74. Robert Caldwell (1814–91) was Bishop of Tinnevelly and co-adjutor to the Bishop of Madras. He was a lover of comparative philology and a great oriental scholar. He published, in 1856, his *Comparative Grammar of the Dravidian and South Indian Family of Languages*. See Sir John Cummings (ed.), *Revealing India's Past* (London, 1939) and P. Carleton, *Buried Empires* (London, 1939).

75. These words are in his article 'The Monuments of Ancient India' in E. J. Rapson (ed.), *The Cambridge History of India*, Vol, I (Cambridge, 1922), p. 612.

76. For modern accounts of the Indus civilization see S. Piggott, *Prehistoric India* (Harmondsworth, Penguin Books, 1950); Sir Mortimer Wheeler, *Early India and Pakistan* (London, revised edn., 1968), *The Indus Civilisation* (Cambridge, 2nd edn., 1960), *Civilizations of the Indus Valley and Beyond* (London, 1966); D. D. Kosambi, *The Culture and Civilisation of Ancient India* (London, 1965); D. H. Gordon, *The Prehistoric Background of Indian Culture* (Bombay, 1958); H. D. Sankalia, *Indian Archaeology Today* (London, 1962).

77. Sir Mortimer Wheeler in Stuart Piggott (ed.), *The Dawn of Civilization* (London, 1961), p. 247.

78. ibid., p. 243.

79. ibid., p. 248. This chapter in *The Dawn of Civilization* was rewritten as *Civilizations of the Indus Valley and Beyond* (London, 1966); see pp. 13, 52, 61–2, and for a further expansion of Wheeler's views see his *Alms for Oblivion* (London, 1966), chapters 3, 4, and 7.

CHAPTER 5

80. Raymond Dawson (ed.), *The Legacy of China* (Oxford, 1964).

81. Sir George Staunton, *Macartney's Embassy to China* ... (London, 1797), Vol. I, p. 27; T. R. Malthus, *First Essay on Population* (reprinted with notes by J. Bonar, London, 1926), p. 335; new edition (ed. A. G. N. Flew), Harmondsworth, Penguin Books, 1971.

82. J. F. Davis, *Chinese Miscellanies* (London, 1815), p. 50.

83. Raymond Dawson (ed.), *The Legacy of China* (see note 80), p. 7.

84. Condorcet, *Sketch for a Historical Picture of the Progress of the Human Mind* (first published 1795; see translation by J. Barraclough, London, 1955), p. 39.

85. Raymond Dawson (ed.), *The Legacy of China* (see note 80), p. 2.

86. William Watson, *China before the Han Dynasty* (London, 1961).

87. B. Laufer, *Publications (Anthropological Series) of the Field Museum of Natural History* (Chicago, 1912), X, p. 71.

88. For summaries of present knowledge on Chinese archaeology see W. Watson, *China before the Han Dynasty* (London, 1961); *Ancient Chinese Bronzes* (London, 1962); *Early Civilization in China* (London, 1965); Chêng Tê-K'un, *Archaeology in China* (Cambridge), Vol I, *Prehistoric China* (1960); Vol. II *Shang China* (1960); Vol. III, *Chou China* (1963); and *New Light on Prehistoric China* (1966); Chang Kwang-chih, *The Archaeology of Ancient China* (New Haven, 1963); W. A. Fairservis, *The Origins of Oriental Civilization* (New York, 1959); Li Chi, *The Beginnings of Chinese Civilization* (Seattle, 1957).

89. J. G. Andersson, *Children of the Yellow Earth* (London, 1934).

90. On the silk route to China see M. P. Charlesworth, *Trade-routes and Commerce of the Roman Empire* (Cambridge, 1924), especially chapter 6; Eileen Power, 'The Opening of the Land Routes to Cathay', chapter 7 in A. P. Newton (ed.), *Travel and Travellers of the Middle Ages* (London, 1930).

91. Childe's views were set out in *Man Makes Himself* (London, 1936), and *What Happened in History* (Harmondsworth, Penguin Books, 1960). For Andersson's views see *Children of the Yellow Earth* (London, 1934), and 'Researches into the Prehistory of the Chinese', *Bulletin of the Museum of Far Eastern Antiquities* (Stockholm), 15, 1943.

92. On oracle-bones see K.-C. Chang, *The Archaeology of Ancient China* (New Haven, 1963), pp. 135–7, and 153–67; Chêng Tê-K'un, *Shang China* (Cambridge, 1960); W. Watson, *Early Civilization in China* (London, 1966), pp. 55–9.

93. Chêng Tê-K'un, *Shang China,* p. 161.

CHAPTER 6

94. For a recent revival of the Madoc myth see Richard Deacon, *Madoc and the Discovery of America* (London, 1967), but also read Thomas Stephens, *Madoc* (London, 1893) and David Williams, *John Evans and the Legend of Madoc* (Cardiff, 1963).

95. For the discovery of American civilization see J. H. Parry, *Europe and a Wider World, 1415–1715* (London, 1949); Gordon Willey in *Peabody Centennial Lectures* (Cambridge, Massachusetts, 1967); Carleton S. Coon, *The History of Man* (London, 1955).

96. On the Maya see Michael D. Coe, *The Maya* (London, 1966); George W. Brainerd, *The Maya Civilization* (Los Angeles, 1954); Sylvanus G. Morley, *The Ancient Maya* (Stanford, 3rd edn., 1956); J. Eric S. Thompson, *The Rise and Fall of Maya Civilization* (Norman, Oklahoma, 1959).

97. On the Incas see Alfred Metraux, *The Incas* (London, 1965); G. H. S. Bushnell, *Peru* (London, revised edn., 1965); Victor W. von Hagen, *Realm of the Incas* (New York, 1957); J. Alden Mason, *The Ancient Civilizations of Peru* (Harmondsworth, Penguin Books, revised edn., 1964).

98. Carleton S. Coon, *The History of Man from the First Human Primitive Culture and Beyond* (London, 2nd edn., 1962), p. 344.

99. For a study of the impact of the discovery of America on European thought see Margaret T. Hogden, *Early Anthropology in the Sixteenth and Seventeenth Centuries* (Philadelphia, 1964); and H. N. Fairchild, *The noble savage: a study in romantic naturalism* (New York, 1928).

100. Jacquetta Hawkes, *The World of the Past* (London, 1963), p. 65.

101. On these matters see R. Wauchope, *Lost Tribes and Sunken Continents* (Chicago, 1962).

102. A good introduction to the Vinland problem can be found in R. A. Skelton, T. E. Marston and G. D. Painter, *The Vinland Map and the Tartar Relation* (New Haven and London, 1965).

CHAPTER 7

103. For up-to-date general summaries of our present knowledge about American prehistory see Gordon R. Willey, *An Introduction to American Archaeology*, Vol. I, *North and Middle America* (Englewood Cliffs, 1966); Henri Lehman, *Les Civilisations Précolombiennes* (Paris, 1961); S. K. Lothrop, *Treasures of Ancient America* (Geneva 1964); G. H. S. Bushnell, *Ancient Arts of the Americas* (London, 1965).

104. See R. S. MacNeish, *First Annual Report of the Tehuacán Archaeological-Botanical Project* (Andover, 1961); *Second Annual Report of the Tehuacán Archaeological-Botanical Project* (Andover, 1962); *Science*, 1964, p. 531; *Antiquity*, 1965, pp. 87–94.

105. For a general summary of modern archaeological knowledge about Peru see G. H. S. Bushnell, *Peru* (London, revised edn., 1965); J. Alden Mason, *The Ancient Civilisations of Peru* (Harmondsworth, Penguin Books, revised edn., 1964); Hermann Leicht, *Pre-Inca Art and Culture* (London, 1960); Wendell C. Bennett and Junius B. Bird, *Andean Culture History* (London, 1960); and P. A. Means, *Ancient Civilizations of the Andes* (New York and London, 1931).

106. In Carl H. Kraeling and Robert M. Adams (eds.), *City Invincible* (Chicago, 1960), p. 55.

107. Michael D. Coe, *Mexico* (London, 1962), p. 84.

108. On Monte Albán see John Paddock (ed.), *Ancient Oaxaca Discoveries in Mexican Archaeology and History* (Stanford, 1968).

109. René Millon, Bruce Drewitt, and James A. Bennyhoff, *The Pyramid of the Sun at Teotihuacan: 1959 investigations*, Transactions of the American Philosophical Society (Philadelphia), 1965, pt 6, p. 55.

110. Michael D. Coe, *The Maya* (London, 1962), p. 168.

111. See J. Eric S. Thompson, *The Rise and Fall of Maya Civilization* (Norman, Oklahoma, 1959); George W. Brainerd, *The Maya Civilization* (Los Angeles, 1954); Sylvanus G. Morley, *The Ancient Maya* (Stanford, 3rd ed., revised Brainerd, 1956).

112. On this see Robert McC. Adams, *The Evolution of Urban Society: Early Mesopotamia and Prehispanic Mexico* (Chicago, 1966).

CHAPTER 8

113. On Jericho see K. M. Kenyon, 'Earliest Jericho', *Antiquity*, 1959, p. 5; *Digging Up Jericho* (London, 1957); *Archaeology in the Holy Land* (London, 1960). The controversy about whether Jericho was a city and was a civilization as Dr Kenyon claims, can be pursued in the pages of *Antiquity*, 1956, pp. 132–6, 184–94, 224–5; 1957, pp. 36–8, 73–84. Gordon Childe denied that it was a city (*Antiquity*, 1957, pp. 36–7), Braidwood reluctantly agreed that it was a town (*Antiquity*, 1957, pp. 74 and 77), while Rushton Coulborn in *The Origin of Civilized Societies* (Princeton, 1959), p. 19, is more sceptical. So am I.

114. G. Glotz, *The Greek City* (London, 1929).

115. Carl Sauer wanted an early centre of agriculture in southeast Asia where dog and pig were domesticated, and the domesticated plants included root crops. See his 'Environment and Culture during the Last Deglaciation', *Proc. American. Phil. Soc.*, 1948, p. 74, and his *Agricultural Origins* (New York, 1952), p. 24. See also Ralph Linton, *The Tree of Culture* (New York, 1964), p. 95; E. Anderson, *Plants, Man and Life* (Berkeley, California, 1968), p. 142; and A. G. Haudricout and L. Hedin, *L'Homme et les plantes cultivées* (Paris, 1948). G. D. Murdock, in his *Africa, its Peoples and their Culture History* (New York, 1959), places the origin of the cultivated sorghums in West Africa near the headwaters of the Niger River where he says there was an independent origin of agriculture.

116. For a good popular statement of the Egyptocentric point of view see the opening words of the 1908 (6th remodelled) edition of Baedeker's *Guide to Egypt*: 'Ever since the attention of the civilized world was redirected to Egypt at the beginning

of the 19th century, the scientific investigation of its innumerable monuments has pointed with ever-growing certainty to the valley of the Nile as the cradle of history and of human culture.' Fifty years before, Kenrick wrote his *Ancient Egypt under the Pharaohs* (1850) and in it he said: 'There is no difficulty in fixing on the country from which Ancient History must begin. The monuments of Egypt, its records and its literature surpass those of India and China in antiquity by many centuries.'

117. The best sources for a critique of the Elliot Smith/Perry hyper-diffusionist doctrine are R. Wauchope, *Lost Tribes and Sunken Continents* (Chicago, 1962); R. B. Dixon, *The Building of Cultures* (New York and London, 1928); R. H. Lowie, *The History of Ethnological Theory* (London, 1937), chapter 10; and G. E. Daniel, *The Idea of Prehistory* (London, 1962), chapter 5.

118. Lord Raglan, *How Came Civilization?* (London, 1939).

119. I have always found one of the most stimulating, fair and clear books on these matters to be R. U. Sayce, *Primitive Arts and Crafts* (Cambridge, 1933).

120. R. von Heine-Geldern (*Paideuma*, IV, 1950, pp. 51–92).

121. *Antiquity*, 1965, pp. 75–6.

122. Betty J. Meggers, Clifford Evans and Emilio Estrada, *The Early Formative Period on Coastal Ecuador: the Valdivia and Machalilla Phases* (Washington, D. C., Vol. I of the *Smithsonian Contributions to Anthropology*, 1965); Betty J. Meggers, *Ecuador* (London, 1966).

123. I did not mention the Kontiki expedition in my lectures, but the subject was often brought up in seminars. The Kontiki expedition is irrelevant to the issue here discussed of trans-Pacific connexions in the west-east direction. What Thor Heyerdahl and his brave colleagues did was to demonstrate that trans-Pacific connexions in an east-west direction were possible, and by means of a balsa raft.

124. J. H. Steward, *Theory of Cultural Change* (Urbana, Illinois 1955).

125. Joseph R. Caldwell in Caldwell (ed.), *New Roads to Yesterday: Essays in Archaeology* (New York, 1966), p. 33.

126. Stuart Piggott, *Ancient Europe* (Edinburgh, 1963), p. 20.

BOOKS FOR FURTHER READING

THE reader who wants to follow up detailed points will be led
to them by the seminar notes. For the general reader who wants
a short list of books to go on to from this present book, the following are recommended:

V. GORDON CHILDE, *What Happened in History* (Harmondsworth, Penguin Books, 1960); *Man Makes Himself* (London, Watts, 1936).

GRAHAME CLARK, *From Savagery to Civilisation* (London,
Cobbett Press, 1946); *World Prehistory* (Cambridge, the Uni-
versity Press, 1961); (with S. Piggott) *Prehistoric Societies* (New
York, Knopf, and London, Hutchinson, 1965); revised editions
London, Hutchinson, 1970 and Harmondsworth, Penguin
Books, 1970.

S. PIGGOTT (ed.), *The Dawn of Civilization* (London,
Thames and Hudson, and New York, McGraw-Hill, 1961).

CARLETON S. COON, *The History of Man* (first published
London, Cape, 1955); revised edition Harmondsworth, Penguin
Books, 1967.

RALPH LINTON, *The Tree of Culture* (New York, Knopf,
1964; with a shortened version in Mentor Books).

RUSHTON COULBORN, *The Origin of Civilized Societies*
(Princeton, the University Press, 1959).

JACQUETTA HAWKES and SIR LEONARD WOOLLEY, *Prehistory and the Beginnings of Civilisation* (London, Allen &
Unwin, 1963: Vol I of the UNESCO *History of Mankind*).

H. FRANKFORT, *The Birth of Civilisation in the Near East*
(London, Williams & Norgate, 1951).

ROBERT McC. ADAMS, *The Evolution of Urban Society:
Early Mesopotamia and Prehispanic Mexico* (Chicago, Aldine,
1966).

R. J. BRAIDWOOD, *The Near East and the Foundations for
Civilization* (Oregon, Eugene, 1952).

INDEX

MORE ABOUT PENGUINS
AND PELICANS

Penguinews, which appears every month, contains details of all the new books issued by Penguins as they are published. From time to time it is supplemented by *Penguins in Print*, which is a complete list of all books published by Penguins which are in print. (There are well over three thousand of these.)

A specimen copy of *Penguinews* will be sent to you free on request, and you can become a subscriber for the price of the postage. For a year's issues (including the complete lists) please send 25p if you live in the United Kingdom, or 50p if you live elsewhere. Just write to Dept EP, Penguin Books Ltd, Harmondsworth, Middlesex, enclosing a cheque or postal order, and your name will be added to the mailing list.

Some other books published by Penguins are described on the following pages.

Note: *Penguinews* and *Penguins in Print* are not available in the U.S.A. or Canada

PREHISTORIC SOCIETIES ~

Grahame Clark
Stuart Piggott

'Brilliant chapters bring prehistoric man to life from the earliest times, when his tools were split pebbles, during the hundreds of centuries in which he was a food collector devising stone and bone implements for the hunt and domestic task, down to his burgeoning as a food-producer' – A. D. Lacaille in the *Tablet*

'Here are Neanderthal and Cro-Magnon, Celts and Achaeans, Iroquois and Eskimos, plentifully illustrated with rock-engravings and the tools our ancestors used in the conquest of their fellow-animals.... Meticulous in avoidance of speculation, it is accurate, up-to-date, readable and full of interest' – *Economist*

'Here is archaeology most brilliantly used for the writing of history' – Jacquetta Hawkes in the *Sunday Times*

a Pelican Original

PRE-CLASSICAL

From Crete to Archaic Greece

John Boardman

The power and personality of King Minos or Agamemnon
are shrouded in legend. But from the art and artefacts that
have survived we can begin to draw pictures of the real
quality of life in the Bronze Age palaces of Crete or
Mycenae, or in the world of Archaic Greece after the Dark
Ages. This book portrays through the forms and subjects
of their art the civilizations that stand at the beginnings
of the Western tradition.

PREHISTORIC CRETE

R. W. Hutchinson

Crete has rightly been called the cradle of European civilization. The Bronze Age Minoans, who were Europe's first city dwellers, had a culture as rich and developed as their great contemporaries in Egypt, Syria, Anatolia, and Mesopotamia.

The thrilling discoveries already made in Crete between 1900 and 1940, as described by Evans and Pendlebury, stirred the imagination of people all over the world. But in the last twenty years archaeologists have greatly extended our knowledge of life in prehistoric Crete.

This book gives a complete account of what is known of the Minoans today – of their origins, clarified by the brilliant work of Ventris and Chadwick in deciphering the Linear B script, their social organization, their trade, their merchant navy, their religion, and their art.

For those who wish to understand the earliest stages of our civilization, the prehistory of Crete will emerge as a vital and a fascinating episode.

a Pelican Original

THE ORIGINS AND GROWTH
OF ARCHAEOLOGY

Glyn Daniel

In about three centuries archaeology has evolved from treasure-hunting and the quaint speculation of antiquarians into a meticulous discipline, absorbing techniques from other sciences in order to extract the maximum information from the slightest evidence. Dr Glyn Daniel has long been regarded as the foremost British historian of archaeology. In this anthology of key writings he illustrates vividly the dramatic development of his subject. The early blunderings are illustrated by the extraordinary exploits of Belzoni, the romance of the heyday of discovery by Schliemann, Evans and Howard Carter. Later chapters document the equally exciting development of systematic excavation and of techniques for precise dating that would once have seemed impossible.